To ███████████ pe/
11/2/009

With admiration.
P + wishes and

warm regards

Herb Alexander

December 12, 1984

73

The Politics
and Economics
of Organized Crime

The Politics
and Economics
of Organized Crime

Edited by

Herbert E. Alexander
University of Southern California

Gerald E. Caiden
University of Southern California

Lexington Books
D.C. Heath and Company/Lexington, Massachusetts/Toronto

Library of Congress Cataloging in Publication Data
Main entry under title:

The Politics and economics of organized crime.

  Bibliography: p.
  1. Organized crime—United States—Addresses,
essays, lectures.   2. Corporations—United States—Corrupt
practices—Addresses, essays, lectures.   3. Commercial
crimes—United States—Addresses, essays, lectures.
4. Corruption (in politics)—United States.   I. Alexander,
Herbert E.   II. Caiden, Gerald E.
HV6769.P65   1985   364.1'06'073   84–48376
ISBN 0–669–09342–4 (alk. paper)

Published simultaneously in Canada
Printed in the United States of America on acid-free paper
International Standard Book Number: 0–669–09342–4
Library of Congress Catalog Card Number: 84–48376

Contents

Preface and Acknowledgments

Organized crime is front-page news only occasionally. When it is, journalists, criminologists, elected officials, and other interested persons participate in lively debate on the subject. It is important to transform debate into the printed word and to extend debate by means of the publication of significant ideas, findings, and conclusions.

Concerns about organized crime have twice prompted faculty at the University of Southern California (USC) to organize a National Conference on Organized Crime. The first conference, held in November 1979, was organized by Michael Aguirre, at that time a lecturer in the Department of History. Aguirre had been an assistant U.S. attorney and assistant counsel to the U.S. Senate Subcommittee on Investigations. The conference, which lasted two days, had thirty-five speakers and panel members and was attended by close to five hundred others.

It was USC's intention that the 1979 conference would be the first of a continuing series held every few years. A much smaller second conference, held in November 1983, was initiated by Herbert Alexander, professor of political science, and Gerald Caiden, professor of public administration, who had participated in the first conference.

The November 1983 conference was conceptualized along different lines. Eight participants were selected to present papers, distributed by mail prior to the conference, for structured discussion, along with personal interactions over a period of a day-and-a-half, to lead to changes and refinements for publication. A small number of invited guests also attended the conference, and their participation and questions made valuable contributions to the finished product.

Follow-up activities are leading to a continuing agenda in the hope that future conferences, built upon proceedings, can be held.

A generous grant, resulting in this book, was made by the Ford Foundation. The coeditors and the chapter authors are grateful for the opportunities provided by the grant. All participants gained much from the experience, and all are grateful for the help provided by the Ford Foundation.

The coeditors appreciate very much the assistance in planning provided by Michael Aguirre and D. Brendan Nagle, chairman of the Department of History at USC.

The project would not have gone forward as smoothly as it did without the skilled efforts provided by Gloria N. Cornette, conference coordinator. Her management of many details saved the authors and editors much time and many problems.

The editors are grateful also to Sherry P. May, dean of the College of Continuing Education, and to her talented colleagues, Christopher J. Stoy and Kay S. Kevorkian, for their assistance in administering the grant and for hosting the conference.

Finally, we thank Margaret N. Zusky, editor of Lexington Books, for her enthusiasm, encouragement, and editorial suggestions, which added immeasurably to the final product.

The Politics
and Economics
of Organized Crime

1

Introduction: Perspectives on Organized Crime

Gerald E. Caiden and
Herbert E. Alexander

Possibly no other social phenomenon in the United States is so steeped in myths and misconceptions as is the subject of organized crime. The fictions portrayed in *The Godfather* and its sequel were stereotypical and served to perpetuate the myth that organized crime in this country is an alien conspiracy run by the Mafia or La Cosa Nostra, a secret society of Sicilian origins, organized into families throughout the country, held together by kinship and cemented by ritual. This Mafia, a confederation of underworld figures, is supposed to be highly structured, cohesive, powerful enough to intimidate and crush any who stand in its way, and very rich, certainly rich enough to head *Fortune's* Five Hundred largest corporations. It is even claimed that the Mafia has arranged the assassination of public figures in the United States and overseas with the active encouragement of secret services that protected it from investigation in these cases.

One can believe in the existence of a secret society with local chapters without believing that it is run on the organizational model of a modern corporation. Some observers strongly believe that the Mafia is an important reality. A better description is summarized in the preamble of the Organized Crime Control Act of 1970:

> Organized crime in the United States is a highly sophisticated, diversified, and widespread activity that annually drains billions of dollars from America's economy by unlawful conduct and illegal use of force, fraud, and corruption; organized crime derives a major portion of its power through money obtained from such illegal endeavors as syndicated gambling, loan sharking, the theft and fencing of property, the importation and distribution of narcotics and other dangerous drugs, and other forms of social exploitation; this money and power are increasingly used to infiltrate and corrupt our dem-

ocratic processes; organized crime activities in the United States weaken the stability of the Nation's economic system, harm innocent investors and competing organizations, interfere with free competition, seriously burden interstate and foreign commerce, threaten the domestic security and undermine the general welfare of the nation and its citizens[1]

Organized crime is no longer the province of B movie gangsters and racketeers. Research has long discredited the Sicilian origins of organized crime by pointing out its existence in North America before any significant Italian immigration and the extent of multiple ethnic participation and succession, particularly Irish and Jewish, and more recently black and Cuban, criminals engaged in the same illegal activities alongside and in competition with Italian-Americans. Other research has long challenged, if not discredited, a supposedly rigid monolithic structure of linked organized criminal activities run by closely knit families disciplined by an identifiable national hierarchy of underworld leaders who are heads of an elaborate crime corporation, by pointing out that no common organizational pattern exists, that many organized criminal groups operate independently, and that the very nature of conspiratorial activities based on mutual trust contradicts the requirements of a rigid bureaucratic framework. Earlier crude methods of enforcement are still utilized but have been superseded in part by sophisticated organizational techniques and nonviolent options within the law. Most important, organized crime is not something confined to odd alienated fringe groups but is ubiquitous, almost part and parcel of the American way of conducting businesses—almost any business, whenever the intent is to cheat the public, market illegal goods and services, and evade the spirit and intent of the law.

Persistence of the Mafia Mystique

The subject of organized crime remains clouded by the Mafia mystique. Even some who are in a position to know better cannot seem to divest themselves of it. The 1967 President's Crime Commission described organized crime as

> a society that seeks to operate outside the control of the American people and their government. It involves thousands of criminals, working within structures as complex as those of any large corporation, subject to laws more rigidly enforced than those of legitimate governments. Its actions are not impulsive but rather the

result of intricate conspiracies, carried over many years and aimed at gaining control over whole fields of activity in order to amass hugh profits.[2]

One of the first actions of the 1983 President's Commission on Organized Crime was to call before it an underworld figure who was supposed to reveal how the Mafia laundered its money through legitimate financial institutions and what it did with its ill-gotten gains. In advance of the hearing, the commission had indicated that an unnamed mob witness would reveal the intricacies of money laundering. But Aladena (Jimmy the Weasel) Fratianno, the underworld informer who claimed he once headed the Los Angeles crime syndicate, testified that he had never heard of gangsters who laundered their money. The commission chairman complained several times during the session that the commission, appointed to wage "a frontal assault on the mob," could not force witnesses to testify without subpoena power.[3] It is inadequate to establish such a commission without providing it with proper tools to do its job; belatedly the Congress provided it broad subpoena power, the right to grant immunity, to jail for contempt, to gain access to bank records, and to use wiretapped information in its investigations.

Laws continue to be framed with the Mafia mystique in mind. So too are organized crime containment strategies that target criminal conspiracies. For instance, the first Organized Crime Drug Enforcement Task Force in south Florida placed more emphasis on drug interdictions, that is, on preventing illegal drugs from entering the country, than on arresting drug traffickers. Other task forces have focused on the leaders of large organizations that control drug importation and distribution networks, not just the traditional organized crime groups but also major motorcycle gangs, street gangs, and illegal dispensers of substantial quantities of prescription drugs. Task forces' distributions of efforts are simply unknown. But even should the task forces succeed in destroying criminal organizations by convicting leading Mafia figures, the potential profits and continuing drug demand and availability may draw others into the business. Reputable lawyers draw big fees for defending major smugglers, enough to be known as drug lawyers for their skill in successfully challenging evidence on technicalities. Many often claim that drug profits are so high that every jailed dealer could easily be replaced by others ready to pick up the business. Thus the task forces claim success in interdiction (carried out by the Customs Service and the Coast Guard), penetrating drug rings, increasing indictments and convictions, and confiscating single shipments. But observers cite sharp increases in heroin traffic and abuse and glut in the cocaine market that has driven prices down, evidencing that the war on drugs is far from being won, especially in efforts against airborne smugglers.

On the Lower East Side of New York City, repeated crackdowns have failed to halt the narcotics business because 70 percent of drug arrests went right back on the street while the collection rate on fines had dropped to 35 percent. The city's chief narcotics prosecutor is recorded as saying, "If police made 10 times as many arrests, and we had 10 times as many prosecutors, it would still be the same thing. The more you arrest, the more they come back. It's like digging a hole in the ocean."[4]

This is a far cry from the popular portrayal of organized crime as a Mafia composed of rival gangsters engaged in interlocking activities of gambling, vice, and politics who hire mercenaries to extend their business profits from the lawlessness. Yet editors pick out criminals with Italian surnames and print stories with dramatic headlines using words such as *mobsters:*

> Peter Licavoli, 81, Reputed Mobster Dies: Became One of the First of Eastern Mafia Element to Move to Arizona
>
> 2 Arrested on Evidence of Drug Lawyer: Alleged Plot to Kill Grandma Mafia Case Witness Was Taped
>
> Judge Tosses Out Racketeer's Term: Prison Board Had Ignored Sentencing Recommendation
>
> Federal Grand Jury Indicts Mobster Spilotro, 17 Others
>
> Philadelphia Bleeds in Fight to Succeed Mafia's "Docile Don"
>
> Mob's Infiltration of Hotel Union Dental Plans Told
>
> Crime Bosses Charged in Vegas Skimming Case
>
> U.S. Smashes $65 Billion Drug Ring Linked to Mafia
>
> Angels Wage Running War with the Law: U.S. Sees Them as Organized Mobsters

Although all of these reports may be true and well founded, they exaggerate a Mafia mystique that is hard for the public to comprehend. Consequently, the public often is indifferent to the activities of organized criminals because organized crime is not perceived as affecting their lives; yet organized crime often penetrates legitimate businesses and involves the whole community. By restricting perceptions of organized crime to Mafia activities, the public fails to see organized crime behind arson, insurance fraud, credit card fraud, bankruptcy fraud, commercial kickbacks, embezzlement, tax violations, check-kiting, housing code violations, deceptive advertising, home improvement schemes, mortgage milking, diploma mills, chain referral schemes, phony accident rings, fradulent operation of banks or savings and loan associations, money order swindles, pilferage, computer bilking, and industrial espionage, all of which have become so common that the public has come to accept them as facts of life and even a way of life for many. This lack of awareness and concern is organized crime's greatest ally. Members of the public may be the victims, but they also are its customers. They are not always aware that their small contributions to seemingly harmless pursuits are recycled into harmful activities that add to the costs of goods and services and, ultimately, taxes.

The underground economy, in which organized crime operates as a significant but relatively small share, has been rising at a much faster rate than the gross national product. By 1983 it had reached perhaps as much as 15 percent of the GNP, with about one-third of all U.S. households having someone working in the underground economy, either holding an extra job or making money off the books, even without revenue lost from illegal activities. Not surprisingly, in view of open bazaars in drugs and other illegal activites,

> New York City is probably the nation's leader in underground economic activity, and off-the-books business pervades virtually every sector of the local economy. For thousands of jobless New Yorkers, the underground is the only place where they can find work; for many small businessmen, it's the only thing between them and bankruptcy court; for others in high-cash businesses, it's the difference between making a decent living and making a bundle.[5]

Millions of Americans hide money from the Internal Revenue Service; cheating on taxes has become more prevalent and even virtually normal business practice; skimming is legion. Illegal activities flourish and spill over into the public sector where some public officials may be tempted to indulge in similar practices and to routinize corruption by expecting bribes, gifts, kickbacks, and services for daily transactions. Eventually the thriving underground economy is explained away as part of the American system of free enterprise, the spirit of entrepreneurship that still thrives among the people, a new set of incentives to work and produce, something that reduces unemployment and poverty and adds to equal opportunity, political stability, social cohesion, and immigrant absorption. Even the illegal activites that are part of the underground economy bring benefits if one ignores their illegality because they provide goods and services people obviously want and are prepared to pay for; they redistribute wealth and income from the haves to the otherwise have-nots; they provide venture capital for risky enterprises with specialized, round-the-clock service in both the dispensation and collection of funds; they provide extraordinary returns for extraordinary performance and subsidize actual living costs of recipients of discounted stolen goods and bartered services. The implication seems to be that the underground economy should be left alone if only because it employs people who otherwise would be unemployed even though they may be employed as loan sharks, racketeers, gamblers, pimps, prostitutes, thieves, fences, arsonists, murderers, drug pushers, con artists, and smugglers.

Correcting Misconceptions

Clearly there is room for many more perspectives on organized crime than the moralistic and legalistic. According to both, organized crime is wrong, should be outlawed, and must be eliminated. Yet organized crime thrives and caters to a rising demand in an affluent society. It assumes many forms, some of which are related to international events and worldwide markets rather than purely domestic circumstances. It is easier to condone in an increasingly permissive society where moral precepts are not so clear as they once were. It attracts all kinds of new entrepreneurs willing to try their luck, both small timers and large investors willing to take risks in defiance of the law and the established order. It ensnares innocent victims who are unaware that they are prey for the unscrupulous and guilty parties who on occasion knowingly combine with criminals, such as judges, court clerks, lawyers, and police officers who themselves may indulge in racketeering, extortion, and bribery to fix cases. It enables illegal profiteers to reinvest in legitimate business, remaining relatively unknown and insulated if they stick to a low-key life-style, and perceived as becoming rich and powerful if they opt for an open life-style. Acting ethically in their private lives but unethically in their businesses, it is hard for anyone to believe that they would be involved in anything illegal; but they are and they act constantly against the public interest. To them, nothing is sacred—not the government, not defense secrets, not public safety, not public health, not young children, not even hapless senior citizens. None is safe from pursuit of the fast illegal buck and the complexity of the phenomenon of organized crime that aids, assists, and protects those who make fast illegal bucks, the realm of the underworld and the corrupted.

This underworld is difficult to research. The problem has been summarized as follows:

> Participants don't want to talk about their activities or admit involvement, if indeed they can even be identified. The organizations that gather systematic data on organized criminal activities are almost exclusively law enforcement agencies whose purpose is to identify and prosecute violations of the law, rather than to provide data banks for social scientists. Even when they allow access to their files, which is rare, the data are not likely to be those the researcher would have chosen.[6]

The Task Force on Organized Crime of the National Advisory Committee on Criminal Justice Standards and Goals bemoaned the fact that

> no reliable research methodology for the study of organized crime— a phenomenon secret in nature and sophisticated in operation— has ever been developed. No national-level group has ever been appointed and empowered to undertake a systematic documentation of the extent of organized crime in the United States on a state-by-state and region-by-region basis.[7]

Although these statements remain true, research proceeds, and researchers provide new insights and fresh perspectives. Occasionally they meet to exchange views and comment on one another's findings. Two such occasions were provided by the University of Southern California, one in 1979 and one in 1983. At both, the participants had quite different views on practically every aspect, whether it was concrete evidence or theories explaining the phenomenon of organized crime. All regarded sources of information as problematic. Law enforcement personnel viewed the whole approach of government to the control of organized crime as disorganized, with too many different agencies duplicating intelligence efforts and jealously guarding their own territories against encroachment. Their general capabilities had been crippled by new laws restricting the gathering of information and protecting individual privacy. Academics and mass media people complained that there were virtually no independent sources. As one recent participant exclaimed, "What we cover is not organized crime—we cover your [police] coverage of organized crime, your results, your investigations, your prosecutorial results." The selective, dramatic, and at times sensational character of these sources make them suspect and academically dubious.

Fortunately the situation is changing, albeit slowly and sporadically. Some independent research is now available, and the second National Conference on Organized Crime at the University of Southern California was able to commission several original papers, grouped broadly into four main perspectives: definitional, economic, political, and public policy. If organized crime is something much bigger than the Mafia, what is it, and where does one draw the boundaries between organized crime and other criminal activites? The literature on organized crime repeatedly complains about the lack of agreement on terms and definitions. For long it has been admitted that there is no acceptable definition, and confusion reigns about what it is they are fighting by those engaged officially in the war against organized crime. Are the targets identifiable conspiracies linked to the Mafia? Or are all illicit enterprises? What about illegal markets? Rackets and racketeers? Groups formed to commit criminal acts? Crimes that are organized? Or crimes committed by members of organized gangs? Public policy in the United States has been focused on organized criminal groups rather than specific illegal markets, the assumption being that

> an organized criminal group is more dangerous than isolated illegal enterprises because it can do many things that less well organized criminal enterprises may fail to do: corrupt public officials, use violence or the threat of violence effectively, and expand into areas that would not otherwise be controlled or influenced by large criminal organizations, including legitimate business.[8]

This means that too much has been concentrated on the character of the criminal and not enough on the nature of the crime, that organized crime has been approached on a case-by-case basis rather than by examining its component parts to forge effective longer-term strategies, and that the money crimes involved have not been effectively investigated and prosecuted. This approach combined with the fragmented nature of government "tends to guarantee that attacks on crime syndicates or other corrupters will be fragmented, that results will be delayed, and that most reform movements can be outwaited."[9]

What Is the Real Target?

The 1976 Task Force on Organized Crime of the National Advisory Committee on Criminal Justice Standards and Goals avoided the issue: "No single definition is believed inclusive enough to meet the needs of the many different individuals and groups throughout the country that may use it as a means to develop an organized crime control effort."[10] Instead it provided an appendix containing various contrasting definitions and proposed description that attempted to "(1) explain something of the nature of organized criminal activity, and (2) dispel some of the myths and eliminate some of the stereotypes surrounding organized crime by indicating what it is not." It listed seven characteristics:

1. Organized crime is a conspiratorial crime.
2. Organized crime has profit as its primary goal.
3. Organized crime is not limited to illegal enterprises or unlawful services but includes sophisticated activities as well.
4. Organized crime is predatory, using intimidation, violence, corruption, and appeals to greed.
5. Organized crime's conspiratorial groups are well disciplined and incorrigible.
6. Organized crime is not synonymous with the Mafia but knows no ethnic bounds.
7. Organized crime excludes political terrorists, being politically conservative, not radical.

This profile still concentrated on the criminals rather than their crimes, and it failed to bring together three essential features of organized crime, only one of which is an organization that supplies illegal goods and services, the other two being a client public that demands such products and a corrupt public officialdom that protects illegal markets.

Although many observers claim that it is futile or illusory to attempt a definition, Michael Maltz in chapter 2, "Toward Defining Organized Crime," is not among them. He points out how a common definition can be of use in ensuring that resources, responsibilities, and penalties can be appropriately allocated. His approach is to review past definitions of organized crime and consider the characteristics that they suggest are associated with this activity: involvement in corruption, use of (or threats of) violence, continuity of criminal activity, hierarchical structure, rigid discipline, involvement in multiple enterprises, involvement in legitimate enterprises, and bonding among its members. He shows that not all of these characteristics are necessarily associated with what we consider organized crime to be, whether the term is applied to traditional groups (such as the Mafia) or newly emerging groups (such as la Nuestra Familia and motorcycle gangs).

Maltz's attention to defining organized crime focuses on those characteristics that distinguish it from ordinary crime, that make it more difficult to combat. One of the main distinguishing characteristics is the economic power an organized group can amass.

Economic Perspective

Economic analysis should reveal in what ways the operations of illegal businesses differ from the conditions of legal businesses. Economic analysis applied to criminal justice concerns is a relatively recent development. Treating the criminal underworld as a special form of business enterprise is a novel approach. Racketeering and the supply of illegal goods and services have been neglected too long by orthodox economists, although many economic and business principles seem to be at work in the underworld as in legitimate business communities. We need to ask, What incentives and disincentives operate in illegal markets? What are the costs and losses in illegal businesses? Who gains and who loses? Who is able to pass on costs, and who is able to keep the profits? What market conditions determine which crimes become organized? Why do criminal enterprises diversify? How do they operate monopolies and cartels? What distinguishes black markets from regular markets? What are the economics of extortion? What are the peculiar characteristics of specific illegal markets? How are illegal markets internally regulated? What keeps organized crime out of some markets but not others? What would happen to consumption (demand) if illegal markets were legalized? Would they be open to more competition, would prices drop, or would illegal entrepreneurs move into more profitable businesses? Few current economic texts seek to answer these questions.

The economic study of illegal enterprise is attracting increasing attention. Three examples of economic research are presented in chapters 3, 4, and 5. In chapter 3, "Money Laundering and the Organized Underworld," Clifford Karchmer deals with the controversial subject of how tainted money generated in illegal markets is converted into acceptable assets that conceal their origin and what measures might be taken to reduce the profits or economic incentives of lucrative illegal activites. Tracing wealth that cannot be accounted for from legitimate sources back to its origins should provide evidence of illegal activities that produce the wealth. Presumably most profits earned in illegal enterprises eventually surface somewhere in the legal economy in the form of legitimate financial instruments. The audit trail should lead back to organized crime and might indicate where the flow could be shut off, thereby making life difficult for criminals. Certainly greater sanctions can be brought than asset seizure and forfeiture, which has so far produced much less than 1 percent of estimated narcotics proceeds. Emphasis on enforcement against laundering denotes inability to control or reduce illegal activities at their source. It is at best a fallback strategy to combat organized crime.

Participants in organized crime have to do something with their money besides sitting on their cash. Their presumed ignorance of laundering and their relative lack of sophistication in choosing options make them vulnerable to audit investigations despite extraordinary precautions taken to shroud their activities in secrecy and to diversify fairly simple financial transactions. Hence, organized crime leaders prefer foreign and offshore banking where secrecy is guaranteed, and they seek to take multiple financial steps that obscure the origins of funds used to acquire assets. Moreover, major unconnected drug dealers are likely to have more money than they can safely handle onshore. Like good capitalists everywhere, they also want to make money from their money, obtaining the best possible returns on their legitimate investments, which in turn makes them vulnerable to audit investigations unless they restrain themselves with lower returns from relatively safe, conservative investments in socially desirable goods. Unfortunately banks are often lax in conforming to currency reporting regulations of the U.S. Treasury, other financial institutions (casinos, commodity exchanges) are exempt from Treasury regulations, and the Treasury itself is slow to record the information. Consequently enforcement agencies resort to more undercover and sting operations to catch the unwary. The need exists to develop better skills in investigations of laundering and to concentrate the use of experienced investigations to the task of improving existing capacity to contain organized crime. However, greater success in combating laundering, which transforms dirty money into clean, may force underground money to seek less socially desirable outlets.

Peter Reuter, in chapter 4, "Racketeers as Cartel Organizers," also examines the involvement of organized crime in the legitimate economy. His specific interest is the set of industries that over a long period of time apparently have been heavily influenced by racketeers. He argues that corrupt unions may be the unique instrument for the exertion of such control; other forms of intimidation are harder to conceal and exert with continued effectiveness. Control of such a union permits the coercion of firms under the guise of labor protection.

What is the optimal strategy for using the coercive power of the corrupt union, taking into account the law enforcement risks and the monetary benefits of the alternative stategies? Reuter argues that it is unlikely to be optimal to attempt to exclude existing competitors and to enfranchise a monopolist, since these actions will generate informative complaints from the firms that are coerced out of the industry. Instead it may be optimal to operate a cartel, with the racketeers being paid to use the union for purposes of enforcing the cartel rule (such as customer allocation) and deterring new entrants. The fact that the racketeers are known to be willing to use force to back up their threats will help ensure that all members of the industry go along with the cartel's rule. The racketeer's reputation will deter new entrants, which makes the cartel still more effective. This analysis suggests the importance of a broad reputation for the control of violence and may explain the observation that racketeer-controlled industries appear to be predominately Mafia influenced since the Mafia has a uniquely strong reputation for the command of violence.

Just how organized crime operates in economic terms in one of these markets is analyzed by Mark Kleiman in chapter 5, "Drug Enforcement and Organized Crime." The author breaks the illegal drug market into its different and distinct component submarkets reflecting the price elasticity of the major drugs: heroin, marijuana, and cocaine. Heroin demand tends to be rather inelastic in the short run because of the habitual nature of heavy users, although it will be less so over the longer term because even the most habitual users will have to cut back on purchases if the price rises steeply. Marijuana demand also appears to be relatively inelastic but for different reasons; its small share of consumer expenditures tolerates price increases even over the long run. Cocaine is price elastic but is a luxury item; heavy users seem to be wealthy people who can afford it, and it retains its attraction as a high-status symbol despite higher prices. Given inelastic demand, a tough law enforcement policy that reduced supply would only generate higher prices, higher revenues, and higher profits for the smaller pool of suppliers. Ironically, with more money at stake there would be more to fight about, more to extort, more to steal, more to guard; violence would probably rise, thereby squeezing out the more pacific suppliers and making the trade even more dangerous. Thus successful drug enforcement will tend to increase levels of violence by both users and traffickers, especially in the short run, though this is likely to be more true for marijuana and less true for heroin. Furthermore it will actually serve organized crime interests by restricting the entry of new criminal empires and increasing the wealth, power, and threat of high-level established dealers. The benefits of decreased drug consumption may not outweigh the costs of increased wealth and power for major dealers in marijuana and cocaine. This suggests that containment should be aimed more at keeping drug dealing out of where it does not now exist, and with lower-level dealers rather than top-level dealers, which in turn would require more nonprison sanctions such as home confinement and community service. A better policy still from the perspective of controlling organized crime would be to reduce demand through public education aimed at the principal users.

Political Perspective

If at times the economic perspective on organized crime comes up with surprising conclusions often at loggerheads with conventional thinking of the more legal approach, the political perspective as presented in chapters 6 and 7 still assumes that organized crime would not exist or persist without official corruption. Economic analysis suggests that organized crime can exist without both. There can be no doubt that organized crime wields illegitimate power. Does it also wield legitimate power by infiltrating and suborning the political system? There are those who believe that organized crime is an integral part of the capitalist system, that the laws are dictated by class interests, that the legal system enforces class interests, and that criminal behavior is best understood in relation to conflicting class interests. Organized crime serves the interests of the governing elites who tend to condone its existence in practice while condemning it in public rhetoric. The governing classes comprise opinion leaders who perpetuate common myths and misconceptions to hide their alliance and mutual dependency and perhaps to use the declared war on organized crime to justify forms of political repression and to appease public sensibilities. In short, "Organized crime is the sum of innumerable conspiracies, most often local in scope, which are part of the social and political fabric of this nation."[11] In this perspective, organized crime in the United States can be seen to wield legitimate power.

This seems credible. In chapter 6, "Organized Crime and Politics," Herbert Alexander gives examples of organized criminal involvement in political campaign financing and in buying favors from office-holders. In a democratic society such as the United States, the wealthy try to influence the course of government, and wealthy crime syndicates are no exception. On the contrary, they have much to gain in penetrating the government in territories where they operate, especially in the big cities where they seem to concentrate, in certain states that seem to indulge them, and in some party machines that they dominate. Alexander admits that "the underworld has ample cash available with which members can and do seek protection, enter legitimate organizations or committees having political interests, insidiously muscle in or seek to influence the political or campaign decision-making processes, even monopolize the political processes in some areas." But nobody knows to what extent. That the political world and the underworld mix cannot be denied. Even the highest public offices are not immune, as illustrated by the 1982 investigation into the U.S. Secretary of Labor Raymond Donovan's alleged links and the resignation of San Diego County Sheriff John Duffy from the President's Organized Crime Commission on the eve of its first public meeting following allegations of his association with reputed organized crime figures.

In chapter 7, "Political Corruption in Small, Machine-Run Cities," David Bellis argues that corrupt machine-run cities should be considered part of organized crime even if they cannot be included in the underworld. They act just like racketeers, the only difference being that they run legitimate organizations. Bellis insists that political corruption becomes organized crime "when there is corruption of public officials, violence or threat of violence in political communities, sophistication in the organization and commission of illegal political acts, continuity in terms of continual illegal acts by public officials in the same community, and some kind of structure under which the crimes are carried out, such as a political machine." He justifies his case with reference to actual circumstances in a small machine-run city in California. He quotes instances of election fraud, illegal zoning, nondisclosure of economic interests, and conflicts of interest by elected officials in that city, and he maintains that his examples are not exceptional but may be quite typical of small, machine-run cities across the nation. He concludes "that the governmental ruling arms of a business-dominated society are loath to intimidate the metabolism of money making, especially their own, with nagging matters of illegalities, proper planning, and the public interest" and laments "that organized crime [may run] America and is such an integral part of this country's political, economic, and social fabric that it will never be obliterated."

Public Policy Perspective

Bellis's pessimism is not shared by those who look at organized crime from a public policy perspective. These too are political realists. They realize that organized crime is embedded in American society, that it meets certain social needs, that it is wealthy and powerful, that prosecuting syndicate heads will not alter the complex circumstances that give rise to illegal enterprise, and that traditional moral-legal sanctions do not fare well in contemporary America. They are prepared to examine the evidence objectively and to consider alternate strategies to dealing with this particular social phenomenon. They will accept different definitions of organized crime and go along with changing perceptions as conditions alter. They will examine the surprising conclusions of economic analysis and weigh them carefully against conventional wisdom. They will take into account the political power, both illegitimate and legitimate, of organized crime. And while they must accept what does not work, they also know what does work and can project what could be made to work better to achieve declared policy objectives.

In chapter 8, "Asset Forfeiture under the Federal Criminal Law," G. Robert Blakey asserts that much more could be done to take the profits out of organized crime by seizing assets presumably obtained through illicit funds. Power to seize assets under the Racketeer Influenced and Corrupt Organizations (RICO) provisions of the Organized Crime Control Act of 1970 and the Continuing Criminal Enterprise provisions of the Comprehensive Drug Abuse Prevention and Control Act of 1970 has been undcrutilized, although historically it has been a traditional instrument in combating economic crimes. The condition may be due to narrow court interpretations and practical obstacles. Actually the language of the statutes is extraordinarily broad and although conceived as a tool for the prosecution of Mafia-type organizations, it can apply to virtually any and every business and commcrical dispute. Once this was realized relatively late in the 1970s, lawyers started adding RICO charges to various types of civil suits. Certain of *Fortune's* top Five Hundred corporations have either accused others of being racketeers or been accused of racketeering themselves. So too have bank customers dissatisfied with loan rates, spouses in alimony disputes, and even an elderly woman who accused her son of diverting her social security checks. The statutes are being applied in ways never envisaged and not for the purpose originally intended. As a result, the legal community is now unsettled over RICO, although Blakey, who was the principal draftsman of the Organized Crime Control Act, has always maintained that it was intended to cover the kind of private litigation now reaching the courts. Although the list of racketeering offenses within RICO included felonies, such as extortion, kidnapping, gambling, arson, and prostitution, usually connected with mobsters, it also included federal mail and wire fraud crimes and the antifraud provisions of federal securities laws. Any single disputed business action that included more than one telephone call or letter can qualify as a RICO case. Thus RICO has drawn attention to questionable business practices of major corporations. Blakey knew at the time that RICO was not limited to organized crime but extended to all businesses that might do some of the same things that mobsters do. RICO's civil provisions have only now become employed largely because young U.S. assistant attorneys familiar with them have been joining private law firms. Despite attempts to alter the provisions so as to lighten its wording and restrict its use, RICO remains available for greater use in prosecuting organized crime.

In a general overview, Gerald Caiden, in chapter 9, "What Should Be Done about Organized Crime?" places the new perspectives themselves into perspective in the continuing debate on containing the growth, wealth, power, and influence of organized crime in American society. We do not know what to do because we do not have enough information, but even if information were available, he says, we are reluctant to choose among alternative policy proposals because we cannot make up our minds about organized crime. Clearly organized crime is a functioning institution, supplying goods and services demanded by society and operating with the occasional connivance of government and law enforcement and tacitly condoned by the American public. The democratic ethos opposes the harsh measures needed to reduce it drastically. Liberals feel that the cure would be as bad as, perhaps worse than, the disease. Nonetheless much more can and should be done within existing guidelines. A national coordinated strategy is needed to replace fragmentary piecemeal efforts. Intelligence activities need to be strengthened along with research, investigating capabilities, and electronic surveillance. The inner workings of specific illegal activities such as bookmaking and arson need to be pinpointed and then countered with appropriately tailored remedies. Highly motivated and informed career professionals have to be retained and their number increased. Probably containment strategies adopted in this country should be integrated and coordinated with an international campaign to reduce harmful illegal businesses that thrive around the world.

Needed: A National Perspective

All the foregoing perspectives are but individual pieces of an elaborate jigsaw puzzle of organized crime, with many pieces still missing and others so scattered that no discernible pattern can be seen. Photographing street walkers plying their trade or junkies making a score, which is fairly easy to do and all too often passes as exposés of organized crime, is not the same as patiently and laboriously tracking prostitutes and junkies to discover whether and how they are organized, who does the organizing, and what the overall pattern looks like. Similarly random apprehension of single boats and planes that carry illegal narcotics is not the same as tracing trade flows, outlining the organization of the trade, and identifying key points and actors. The pattern is the key to proper understanding. This kind of overall appreciation of the nature of organized crime is largely lacking in the United States. No wonder that the 1967 Report of the Task Force on Organized Crime stated that there was (and still is) no agreement on defining the problem, insufficient data on which to assess the problem, unwillingness to share what data exist, no national leadership in tackling the problem, no national strategy, no agreement on standards, no cooperation among public authorities, no dedicated public and private commitment to solve the problem, no reliable research methodology even to study the problem.[12] The task force outlined a comprehensive national program to remedy these shortcomings, but it still made the mistake of combining forms of organized crime and intimating that a common strategy would be effective in tackling all of them. This might be true if organized crime were small-time, nonviolent, or marginal, but by the report's own admission, it was none of these. It also might be true if organized crime was organized by the same people in one large interconnected structure, but again the report's findings suggest otherwise.

If there is one theme that runs through exposees on organized crime in the United States, it is that few seem to care enough to seize the initiative and be able to assume national leadership. Has organized crime so entrenched itself in American society that it has become a permanent fixture? Has it become so proficient in doing what it does that it has become indispensable? Has it grown so big that too many people are caught up in it? Has it penetrated so deeply into public life that it can block any serious threat made against it? Has it already gnawed away at American society that the national will to act has been weakened too much? Has its corrupting influence poisoned civic consciousness? Was Lincoln Steffens right when he commented at the turn of the century that "the spirit of graft and of lawlessness is the American spirit"?[13] Or has organized crime been tamed? Do we overdramatize it? Is it sometimes more efficient to tolerate certain kinds of organized crime than to take action? Is organized crime on the way to being rendered harmless as the dynamics of its own political economy triumphs?[14]

Few can cast stones at others, for if all of us were to look into our own attitudes, behavior, and conduct, we would find something that, if not actually promoting organized crime, does nothing to stop it either. Whether we are aware of organized crime, somehow we all get caught up in it and thus unintentionally become part of it. If we do not like that thought, then we will have to change our laws rather dramatically and our ethical codes or reconstruct our vision of the good society.

Notes

1. Organized Crime Control Act of 1970, p. 1073.

2. President's Commission on Law Enforcement and Administration of Justice, *Task Force Report: Organized Crime* (Washington, D.C., Government Printing Office, 1967), p. 1.

3. Robert Dallos, "Crime Panel's Witness Doesn't Have Answers to Questions on Money," *Los Angeles Times*, March 15, 1984, p. 14.

4. Bob Drogin, "New York's Bazaar: Getting High on the Lower East Side," *Los Angeles Times*, January 8, 1984, p. 18.

5. E. Tivnan, "Cashing In: Life in the Underground Economy," *New York Magazine*, March 21, 1983, p. 26.

6. Annelise G. Anderson, *The Business of Organized Crime* (Stanford, Calif.: Institution Press, 1979), p. 147.

7. Report of the Task Force on Organized Crime, *Organized Crime* (Washington, D.C.: Law Enforcement Assistance Administration, 1976), p. 3.

8. Anderson, *Business*, p. 3.

9. Report of the Task Force on Organized Crime, *Organized Crime*, p. 29.

10. Ibid., p. 7.

11. Alan A. Black and William J. Chambliss, *Organized Crime* (New York: Elsevier, 1981), p. 210.

12. Report of the Task Force on Organized Crime, *Organized Crime*, pp. 1–3.

13. Lincoln Steffens, *The Shame of the Cities* (New York: Hill and Wang, new ed., 1975), p. 9.

14. Albert Fried suggests that it is "the tendency of the American eco-

nomic and political system to (a) force the criminals to play by the rules and in so doing (b) make them ex-criminals sooner or later. Even if the worst is imagined . . . the fact remains that the company must still be run as a business, profits must still be earned, stockholders satisfied, and the regulations laid down by a plethora of government agencies observed. In the end the system swallows up the gangsters in its gigantic maw, leaving behind only the traces of their errant careers." *The Rise and Fall of the Jewish Gangster in America* (New York: Holt, Rinehart and Winston, 1980), pp. 280–281.

2
Toward Defining Organized Crime

Michael D. Maltz

> We have often heard it maintained that sciences should be built up on sharply defined basic concepts. In fact no science, not even the most exact, begins with such definitions. The true beginning of science actually consists rather in describing phenomena and then in proceeding to group, classify and correlate them.
>
> S. Freud

After more than sixty years of contending with organized crime, there is still no adequate definition of it despite many attempts (Maltz 1976; National Advisory Committee 1976; Blakey, Goldstock, and Rogovin 1978). Probably the primary reason for defining organized crime is to determine how resources could be allocated more effectively in attacking it. For example, the U.S. General Accounting Office (GAO) (1977), in passing judgment on the Justice Department's Organized Crime Strike Forces, was critical of the fact that the Justice Department had not defined organized crime, although millions of dollars had been spent by the strike forces to combat organized crime. Congressional hearings and presidential commissions had addressed themselves to this issue, as have research programs. Yet as the GAO pointed out, organized crime was still unabated.

Another reason for defining organized crime is legal. If a specific penalty, for example, obtains for a person convicted of an offense when the offense is considered an organized crime, there should be

This chapter is based on research performed under grant 80-IJ-CX-0066 from the National Institute of Justice, U.S. Department of Justice, to the Temple University Law School. Points of view or opinions expressed in this chapter are those of the author and do not necessarily reflect the official position or policies of the U.S. Department of Justice, the University of Illinois, or Temple University.

some means of distinguishing organized-crime-related offenses from those not involving organized crime. The idea of a prosecutor's appearing before the judge at sentencing and intoning, "This person is a member of organized crime," as justification for an extended sentence does not appear to be just. There should be standards and criteria that could be incorporated into a statute.

A third reason for defining organized crime is for territorial purposes. There are fourteen federal Organized Crime Strike Forces in the United States, all located cheek by jowl with offices of the U.S. Attorney. All of them work in concert with criminal justice agencies at state and local levels. Are there any criteria for deciding whether a given case should be investigated and prosecuted by federal and not state or local agencies when all agencies can rightfully claim jurisdiction? Are there any criteria for deciding whether the appropriate federal prosecutorial agency is the U.S. attorney office or the Organized Crime Strike Force?

Obviously no single definition will solve resource allocation and evaluation issues, legal problems, and jurisdictional disputes, but these needs should be kept in mind when attempting to define organized crime.

Some Current Definitions

Difficulties in defining organized crime can be illustrated by considering some current definitions employed in statutes. The only definition of organized crime in federal statutes is found in public law 90-351. The Omnibus Crime Control and Safe Street Act of 1968:

> Organized crime means the unlawful activities of members of a highly organized, disciplined association engaged in supplying illegal goods and services, including but not limited to gambling, prostitution, loan sharking, narcotics, labor racketeering, and other unlawful activities of such associations.

The vagueness and circular reasoning in this definition are striking. First, if defines organized crime not so much in terms of unlawful activities as in terms of who is committing those unlawful activities. It is an ad hominem definition. Second, it lists a number of unlawful activities, but these are not necessarily the ones that make up organized crime. To determine whether a given activity is an organized crime, one has to:

1. Find an "association engaged in supplying illegal goods and services, including but not limited to gambling, prostitution, loan sharking, narcotics, labor racketeering and other such unlawful activities.
2. Determine whether it is "a highly organized, disciplined association."
3. If the individual in question is a member of this association and if he or she has committed an unlawful activity, that activity (it need not be one of the listed activities) is ipso facto an organized crime.

The federal definition is not used for legal, jurisdictional, or resource allocation purposes. Few can be. For example, in 1975 the law creating New York State's Organized Crime Task Force was declared unconstitutional by the New York State Supreme Court because it did not define organized crime.[1] It is interesting to note that the federal Organized Crime Control Act of 1970 (PL 91-352), passed two years after the Safe Streets Act, did not use the aforementioned—or any other—definition of organized crime. Since then some states have developed definitions for their own purpose. Of particular interest is Ohio's definition:

> "Organized criminal activity" means any combination or conspiracy to engage in criminal activity as a significant source of income or livelihood, or to violate or aid, abet, facilitate, conceal, or dispose of the proceeds of the violation of, criminal laws relating to prostitution, gambling, counterfeiting, obscenity, extortion, loan sharking, drug abuse or illegal drug-distribution, or corruption of law enforcement officers or other public officers, officials, or employees. [National Advisory Commission 1976:215]

This definition no longer focuses solely on the substantive violation of the law but includes any activity related to the violation; however, it is very specific in the substantive offenses that are included and excludes, for example, arson, hijacking, murder, and labor racketeering.

In an earlier attempt to define organized crime, I too was somewhat off the mark (Maltz 1976). My focus was on the fact that many organized crimes exist, and the English language is misused if only certain types of organized crime are considered organized crime. The taxonomy of organized crimes I listed was useful but limited. Most organized crimes in that taxonomy require organization in the commission of the crime—stolen car rings, gambling, price fixing, and so on—whereas many organized crimes are organized not so much in their commission as in the subsequent actions—distribution of the stolen goods through retail outlets, a network of associates and colleagues to help in special circumstances, and even financial and psychological support systems. Organized criminal activity of this nature cannot be included in a taxonomy that focuses only on organized illegal acts because it ignores those organized actions and processes that facilitate the commission of future crimes or improve the felon's situation after committing the crimes. To understand organized crime in all its manifestations, the associated activities that take place well before or well after the crime must be understood and included.

I doubt whether it is worthwhile to attempt to define organized crime generally. One such definition could be "crime that is organized," which does not advance us much.[2] Instead we should focus on the nature of those criminal enterprises agreed to by most observers to be part of organized crime. To distinguish between the generic or general organized crime and the brand name or specific organized crime group, the latter will be italicized.

Characteristics of Organized Crime

In defining organized crime, we can characterize other proposed definitions. Among the characteristics they suggest are the following: corruption, violence, sophistication, continuity, structure, discipline, multiple enterprises, and involvement in legitimate enterprises. Another element considered is the bonding ritual, such as those reported to have been used in making members of the Mafia, La Cosa Nostra, La Nuestra Familia, and the Hell's Angels. These nine possible characteristics should be examined in the context of all types of organized crime, not just of Mafia-like groups but of newer and emerging groups as well. Some appear to be central to the concept of organized crime, while others are peripheral or refer to only one manifestation of it.

Corruption

Corruption is used by criminal organizations to permit them to gain a competitive edge (such as by having construction contracts thrown their way) or to protect themselves from arrest. *Organized crime* almost always involves corruption, although organized crime may not. For example, the Black Hand societies at the turn of the century—and the Blackstone Rangers more recently—were organized extortion rings, but corruption was not the means by which security was achieved. The other parties in the transactions, the victims of extortion, were told in no uncertain terms what would happen to them, their families, and their businesses if they assisted the police. The fact that for the most part the extorted businessmen were members of ethnic groups that at the time did not place much trust in the police also helped maintain the practice. Businessmen were afraid to cooperate with the police.

As these criminal groups evolved and matured, they developed enterprises that dealt in illegal goods and services, in which the other parties to the transactions, the purchasers of illegal goods and services, wanted to keep their involvement secret. In contrast with the previous example, these parties did not want the police to know but if caught were often turned into informers and did cooperate with the police.

The two situations were not completely analogous. In the first case, the parties were usually reputable businessmen who had much to lose if the extorters carried out their threats; in the second case, the parties were often drug addicts and petty criminals with little to lose from those against whom they informed. Because of this greater exposure to arrest and conviction, organized crime groups dealing in these areas find it more expedient to make payoffs to police, prosecutors, and judges than to attempt to keep all their customers in line. Customers have little to lose by informing, but a corrupt official has a great deal to lose if his or her involvement becomes known.

It is usually implicitly assumed that the term *corruption* refers only to public officials who violate their oaths of office; however, corruption of nongovernmental employees is also used to protect schemes from exposure. Bank officials may use their discretionary authority to approve loans for which stolen securities are used as collateral. They may break the law by camouflaging or not recording transactions they are legally required to report (such as large cash transactions) in order to protect *organized crime* schemes. Airport personnel may alter records of flights or may assist in the shipment of contraband. Buyers for department stores and discount houses may alter records of purchases to permit stolen merchandise to be comingled with legally purchased merchandise, or they may buy merchandise at a premium price from an *organized crime*–connected business. In all of these cases, the individuals are acting corruptly in that they are being paid to violate the trust placed in them by their employers. Insofar as the corrupt individuals are concerned, there is no difference between public and private corruption; in both cases, they are using their positions of authority within their organizations to make money in ways inimical to the interests of their employers.

When individuals working for a private business take payoffs in violation of the trust placed in them by their employer, the effects are felt primarily in that particular business (although competitors may also be affected). When individuals working for a public agency take payoffs, that harms the integrity of government—and affects everybody. Some years ago the director of the Financial Crimes Bureau of the Illinois Attorney General's Office was asked in a class of mine about immunity. Why was the industrialist who bribed a half-dozen legislators granted immunity in return for his testimony against them when he was the one who initiated the bribes in the first place? Shouldn't he have been the one to be prosecuted? The director first gave a practical reason. When the industrialist's lawyer learned of the investigation, he brought his client in to make a deal. There would have been no case against anyone had the industrialisit not come forward. There were other strong reasons why this offer was acceptable to the prosecutors. Because the goal of private businesses is to make a profit, it should be expected that some business people resort to illegal practices on occasion. The goal of government is to establish justice, to make sure that illegal practices do not go unpunished. If the integrity of government is threatened, such illegal practices might become the norm. Furthermore money is frequently offered to public officials in return for votes, decisions, contracts, and other favors. If officials are put on notice that bribers may be granted immunity from prosecution if they turn the officials in—and that serious enforcement efforts are underway—even the most corrupt officials will give pause before accepting a bribe. Thus prosecuting the officials was expected to have a greater deterrent effect than prosecuting the industrialist.

Only public sector corruption should be considered an element of organized crime. Whether it is a necessary element is an open question.

Violence

Some types of crimes require violence or the threat of violence for their commission; others do not. But even if an *organized crime* group engages only in victimless crimes, even if it has both a monopoly in its enterprises and docile, stable employees, customers, and associates, violence may be required to keep both competition and rebellion down.

One might think that an *organized crime* group can maintain itself without violence if the group's political or economic power is sufficient; after all, perhaps it does not need to resort to physical power to protect itself once it matures. Yet physical power is almost always necessary. Disputes continually arise within and between organizations. If they cannot be settled by the disputants, coercion must be used. In the upperworld, the legal system is used to settle disputes and is backed by the legal and overt use of coercive force— judicial orders, injunctions, judgments, sentences, and so on. But these are unavailable to organized crime groups. Instead they use criminal and violent force: shootings, beatings, threats of violence. This suggests that the potential for violence is always present in an organized crime group (Dintino and Martens 1981).

Sophistication

Many descriptions of organized crime imply that it is a sophisticated operation. Here the term is taken to mean that illegal enterprises are not run blatantly and that the actors are familiar with the rules of criminal procedure and how to use them to their advantage. Thus, telephone conversations between participants are likely to be in code; illegal goods are rarely handled by the principals; dummy corporations are established and run ostensibly by nominees; paper trails are lengthy and ambiguous. That many *organized crime* organizations may engage in some criminal activities of this sort is very likely the case. But sophistication is not always present. An *organized crime* group engaged in the traditional activities of gambling, prostitution, loan-sharking, and narcotics may be very unsophisticated in operation. Most of the *organized crime* groups that come to the attention of strike forces engage in a number of sophisticated activities, but this is not invariably the case.

Continuity

There are many noncontinuous *organized crime* enterprises. Targets of opportunity arise from a number of situations. For example, a businessman's gambling debts may result in his business being turned over to his *organized crime* debtors, who then pull a bankruptcy scam. They use his credit to order merchandise, sell it below cost and keep the money, and then declare bankruptcy after all other assets have been sold off. This is a one-shot, noncontinuous operation.

Can one envision an *organized crime* group that relies entirely on noncontinuous separable operations like this? Such a group might join forces to plan and execute a major crime and then disband until another opportunity arises. If such a group exists, it may be an organized crime group, but it is not an *organized crime* group. Even if group members engage in different types of crimes—first a hijacking, then a bankruptcy scam, then a securities theft—the crimes are still separate and for the most part can be investigated and prosecuted separately. This suggests that one of the cohesive elements of an organized crime group may be a continuing enterprise, such as drug distribution, extortion, or gambling.

Structure

An *organized crime* group is, of course, organized. But how organized would one ordinarily expect it to be? For example, Cressey's (1969) definition of *organized crime* implies that the organization has a very elaborate formal structure. He specifies that it has "an established division of labor" and "position[s]" for a corrupter, a corruptee, and an enforcer. It seems highly unlikely that such roles are truly as formal as Cressey implies. Although some *organized crime* groups may be this formal, with organization charts and the like, it is doubtful that this is common practice. There may be individuals who corrupt, who are corrupted, and who enforce in support of a particular criminal enterprise, but their roles may change for other enterprises. Studies of particular criminal organizations (Ianni 1972; Anderson 1979) bear out the contention that relationships are often task dependent and changeable.

But even while questioning the utility of basing a definition of *organized crime* on a particular structure, one usually finds a great deal of structure in organized crime groups. They often have a well-defined (if informal) hierarchy, which is maintained by force or other means. On the other hand, predicating a definition on structure would not be particularly useful since one would need to determine the nature of the structure (which may be quite fluid) to prove that a particular manifestation of organized crime is *organized crime*.

Discipline

The reputation that *organized crime* groups have for discipline within their ranks has been eroded considerably over the past two decades.

Joseph Valachi's testimony (Maas 1968), Vincent Teresa's disclosures (Teresa 1973), Jimmy Fratianno's story (Demaris 1981), Gay Talese's book on Bill Bonanno (Talese 1971), and the Gallo-Profaci "war" in the 1960s, among other confessions and events, have demonstrated that discipline within *organized crime* groups has been less than rigid.

One should not expect otherwise. When all individuals in a group are armed and have no compunction about using their weapons—which may be one of the criteria for acceptance by the group—then the ability to govern them must depend to a great extent on the consent of the governed. Discipline of a group's members can be maintained only if it is shown to be in their own self-interest. Although there must be some discipline (just as there must be some structure) in order to consider a particular collection of individuals an organization, it may not play an important part in defining *organized crime.*

Multiple Enterprises

There are many reasons why a criminal organization would diversify its activity beyond a single criminal enterprise. A business that is dependent on only one good or service faces greater risk than one with a number of product lines. For example, a pesticide or fungus could destroy a year's poppy or coca or marijuana crop. Improved drug detectors or other enforcement action might close down the only supply route (suggesting that there should be diversity in supply routes as well). If the profits are high, others will be induced to compete for a share of the market. Or a substitute product may steal most of the market for the product. By diversifying, a business hedges its bets.

But there are advantages to concentrating on a single product. All of the effort is expended in making sure that the product meets the needs of clients. The businessman becomes a specialist. He is intimately familiar with enforcement mechanisms used to investigate his operation. He needs to monitor the efforts of only one or two enforcement units (for example, the state and local vice units, for gambling) instead of a dozen or more if a number of diverse activities are engaged in. And he keeps a lower profile by restricting himself to one enterprise.

It is this last fact—that a criminal organization engaged in only one enterprise has a lower profile—that leads one to conclude that an *organized crime* group must normally be involved in many enterprises; otherwise it would be only an organized crime group. But there may be exceptions, based on organizational scale and on the means used to maintain the enterprise. Consider the hypothetical case of a single organization without any other business tha controls the distribution of an illegal drug, such as heroin, over a sizable territory. The scale of this organization clearly brands it as organized crime (and a strike force responsibility). Of course, to control all distribution of an illegal commodity in a region requires a great deal of organizational ability and a great deal of corruption. With all of the corruption necessary, it would be surprising if the organization did not expand into other areas. Having developed a profitable connection, it is highly unlikely that it would not be exploited to the fullest. For example, in "Wincanton"—Reading, Pennsylvania—Gardiner (1970) shows how the Stern syndicate, whose main business was gambling, branched out into fixing city contracts, zoning and licensing, and prostitution because it had strong corrupt links to the city's government.

Another possible exception to diversity in organized crime might occur if a major legitimate organization is being run criminally. The most obvious example is the International Brotherhood of Teamsters. The prosecutorial effort waged against Jimmy Hoffa in the 1960s by the Justice Department was tantamount to a strike force operation (Brill 1978). Even when only union-related crimes are involved (such as sweetheart contracts, theft of pension funds, threatening rivals in union elections), such activities might well constitute *organized crime* because of the scale of the enterprise. A union as strong as the Teamsters exerts a powerful influence on day-to-day commerce. When officials of even only one local are involved in union-related crimes, they can have a profound effect on the industry in the region because of their almost total control of trucking. The statement that "there is no industry today that can carry on its business if the Teamsters lay down their reins," made by a union leader in 1902, is still true today (Brill 1978).

The issue underlying the characteristic of multiple enterprises, then, seems to be the power and influence exerted by the group, and not the number or diversity of enterprises. By analogy, suppose one person owned a hospital, a nearby pharmacy, a free clinic, and a medical testing laboratory. And suppose a second person owned four hospitals in four different cities, four pharmacies in other cities, four clinics in yet other cities, and four labs in still other cities. The second person would be wealthier overall, but the first person's influence and control over the market for medical services in the area would be considerably greater. A large number of separate and distinct enterprises does not have the clout of a small number of enterprises that are tied to each other.

Legitimate Business

Many have decried the "penetration of legitimate business by organized crime" (Bers 1970) because of the deleterious effect that an *organized crime* group can have on their competitors and customers. Organized crime often does not play by the rules, preferring to use force and violence in place of standard business practices to maximize profits.[3] Pressures of both a business and nonbusiness nature are felt by organized crime groups to become involved in legitimate enterprises. For one, the group may have started out primarily in legitimate business, gravitating to criminal activity because of the greater potential for profits.[4] The *organized crime* group may also get into legitimate business as payment, for example, for gambling or loan shark debts.

And there are other reasons. Legitimate businesses can be used to launder money. By declaring that the business earned more than it actually did, an individual making most of his money illegally can attribute part of it to the business and thus spend it openly without running afoul of the Internal Revenue Service. Legitimate businesses also serve as fronts in another way. Stolen merchandise can be laundered by comingling it with legally purchased merchandise; if the goods have no identifiers (examples are a truckload of meat, razors, or cigarettes), there is no way of tracing the goods to a theft. This has the added advantage of cutting business costs, giving the business an unfair advantage over its competitors.

Another reason for an *organized crime* group's entry into legitimate business is to gain respectability. *Organized crime* has been called "the queer ladder of social mobility" (Bell 1961), a short-cut to success American style for groups without access to the legitimate means of power. Although social status in this country is based primarily on wealth, wealth due to criminal activity does not bring the respectability that legally earned money does. Other family members often feel the social stigma more keenly than the member of the *organized crime* group and bring pressure on him to assume a cloak of respectability.

Thus there are many reasons for an *organized crime* group to diversify into legitimate business. In fact, they are so strong and numerous that one is inclined to believe that an *organized crime* group will always have legitimate enterprises, but experience does not necessarily bear this out. The Hell's Angels, Blackstone Rangers, and La Nuestra Familia may have been considered *organized crime* groups before they became involved in legitimate business (or regardless of such involvement). Furthermore, by suggesting that involvement in legitimate business is a necessary condition, one runs the risk of overlooking emerging *organized crime* groups that may have no legitimate activity.

Bonding

Many *organized crime* groups have rituals that appear to be a combination of mysticism, fraternity initiation rites, and the process of being made a partner in a law firm. The financial aspects of partnership are the driving force for wanting to become a made man, but what about the ritualistic folderol? Is it a necessary concomitant of an *organized crime* group?

First, let us consider the reasons that may underlie the rituals. They may exist to lend an air of legitimacy and romance to the group's criminal activity by attempting to redefine vicious people and acts as part of a larger revolt against society. This can result in a feeling of "It's us against them" or "We'll show them what happens when they exclude us." Another possible reason for the bonding ritual is to keep those on the lower rungs of the organization a goal in line while they work their way up to full membership. In addition, while lip-service may be paid to the idea of brotherhood among the "made" members, the ritual may serve to make more palatable the fact that those at the top rule. In other words, the bonding ritual may be a scam to make people feel that they belong. This was evidently at work in one of the sting operations in Washington, D.C. The thieves who frequented the police-run fencing operation were arrested while they eagerly awaited the appearance of "the don" from New York.

That the bonding ritual exists in Mafia families has been amply documented. Nevertheless, it is not necessarily an attribute of all *organized crime* groups. Even if all such groups in the United States do have some form of ritual associated with them, it is possible to conceive of a group that does not need them.

Conclusion

To recapitulate, the following attributes have been considered as potential indicators of *organized crime:* corruption, violence, sophistication, continuity, structure, discipline, multiple enterprises, legitimate business, and bonding. Corruption, violence, continuity, and involvement in multiple enterprises may be characteristic of essentially all *organized crime* groups; that all have of necessity some structure but no particular structure characterizes all possible *organized crime* groups; that most if not all are engaged in legitimate businesses as well as criminal enterprises, but this may not be a necessary characteristic; and that sophistication, discipline, and bonding may be characteristic of some *organized crime* groups but are neither necessary nor typical.

More time has been spent on determining the characteristics of *organized crime* groups than on the characteristics of *organized crime.* This reflects the ambivalence discussed elsewhere (Maltz 1976): is organized crime an act or a group? Previously I concentrated on the acts, thus leaving out the thread that ties the acts together, the group. This present discussion suggests that *organized crime* cannot be defined based on acts alone; it must also refer to the people who work together as a group to commit them.

There appears to be thread linking the attributes that have been rejected as determinants of *organized crime:* discipline, sophistication, and bonding. They are all characteristics of the archetypical Mafia family. This image of *organized crime* is so powerful that it often blinds us as to other potential forms of *organized crime* groups. They can start out as legitimate businessmen, as a collection of burglars, as a guerrilla or resistance unit, or even as a group of military or police personnel. Perhaps France's OAS (secret army organization), which robbed banks as well as assassinated its enemies, could be considered an organized crime group. Even though its raison d'être was to save France from the disgrace of granting independence to Algeria, its activites went far beyond mere political action. And the SDECE, France's equivalent of the CIA, was deeply implicated in heroin traffic throughout the world (McCoy 1973), of which the French connection was a major aspect.

Definitions that are too broad (for example, *"organized crime* is crime that is organized") are not helpful because there is not enough discrimination. Definitions that are too narrow (for example, *"organized crime* is the Mafia") are not helpful because they are merely ad hominem. We need something more balanced based on the characteristics I have listed here.

Notes

1. This was later reversed by the New York Court of Appeals because the term was used only to determine whether the Organized Crime Task Force had jurisdiction in the case, not whether the acts specified constituted "organized crimes." The court recognized the inherent vagueness in the term, stating, "The phrase 'organized crime activities' is itself not susceptible to precise judicial definition."

2. Commenting on the definition of organized crime used by Arizona, Edelhertz et al. (1981:2) note, "Its defect is that it encompasses a very broad range of the criminal universe. Its virtue is that it permits flexibility of approach with respect to new and developing forms of criminal group activity and encourages attention to emerging groups."

3. This is not to say that legitimate businessmen always play by the rules. Sutherland (1949) pointed this out over thirty years ago, and it is still true (Clinard et al. 1979). However, there is a limit to the extent that they bend or break the rules. *Organized crime* groups often do not even give lipservice to the laws governing business behavior. Customers or competitors are routinely threatened, for example. Involvement in *organized crime* is not the best training ground for a businessman.

4. We normally think of *organized crime* groups as starting out as criminal gangs and then maturing into *organized crime* syndicates. This is not always the case; see Albini (1971) for some counterexamples.

References

Albini, Joseph L. 1971. *The American Mafia: Genesis of a Legend*. New York: Appleton-Century-Croft.

Anderson, Annelise G. 1979. *The Business of Organized Crime: a Cosa Nostra Family*. Stanford, Calif.: Hoover Institution Press.

Bell, Daniel. 1961. "Crime as an American Way of Life." In Bell, Daniel, *The End of Ideology*. New York: Collier.

Bers, Melvin K. 1970. *The Penetration of Legitimate Business by Organized Crime: An Analysis*. Washington, D.C.: Law Enforcement Assistance Administration, April.

Blakey, G. Robert; Ronald Goldstock; and Charles H. Rogovin. 1978. *Rackets Bureaus: Investigation and Prosecution of Organized Crime*. Washington, D.C.: National Institute of Law Enforcement and Criminal Justice, March.

Brill, Steven. 1978. *The Teamsters*. New York: Simon and Schuster.

Clinard, Marshall B.; Peter C. Yeager; Jeanne Brisette; David Petrshek; and

Elizabeth Harris. 1979. *Illegal Corporate Behavior.* Washington, D.C.: National Institute of Law Enforcement and Criminal Justice.

Cressey, Donald R. 1969. *Theft of the Nation: The Structure and Operations of Organized Crime in America.* New York: Harper and Row.

Demaris, Ovid. 1981. *The Last Mafioso.* New York: Times Books.

Dintino, Justin J., and Frederick T. Martens. 1981. "The Process of Elimination: Understanding Organized Crime Violence." *Federal Probation Quarterly* 45(June):26–31.

Edelhertz, Herbert; Bonnie Berk; Roland J. Cole; Marilyn Walsh; and Barbara Keen. 1981. *The Containment of Organized Crime: A Report to the Arizona Legislative Council.* Seattle, Wash.: Battelle Human Affairs Research Centers, December.

Gardiner, John A. 1970. *The Politics of Corruption: Organized Crime in an American City.* New York: Russell Sage Foundation.

Ianni, Francis A.J. 1972. *A Family Business: Kinship and Social Control in Organized Crime.* New York: Russell Sage Foundation.

Kaplan, Abraham. 1964. *The Conduct of Inquiry.* San Francisco: Chandler.

Maas, Peter. 1968. *The Valachi Papers.* New York: G.P. Putnam's Sons.

McCoy, Alfred W. 1973. *The Politics of Heroin in Southeast Asia.* New York: Harper & Row.

Maltz, Michael D. 1976. "On Defining 'Organized Crime': The Development of a Definition and a Typology." *Crime and Delinquency* 26(July):338–346.

National Advisory Committee on Criminal Justice Standards and Goals. 1976. *Organized Crime: Report of the Task Force on Organized Crime.* Washington, D.C.: Government Printing Office.

Sutherland, Ernest H. 1949. *White Collar Crime.* New York: Dryden Press.

Talese, Gay. 1971. *Honor Thy Father.* Greenwich, Conn.: Fawcett.

Teresa, Vincent. 1973. *My Life in the Mafia.* New York: Doubleday.

U.S. General Accounting Office. 1977. *War on Organized Crime Faltering— Federal Strike Forces Not Getting the Job Done.* Report GGD-77-17, Washington, D.C.: General Accounting Office, March 17.

3
Money Laundering and the Organized Underworld

Clifford L. Karchmer

Accorording to recent estimates, illicit drug trafficking and organized crime activities in the United States generate between $30 billion and $100 billion annually in profit.[1] Estimated income from illegal narcotics importing, wholesaling, and street-level sales was between $22 million and $89 billion in 1981. Earnings from illegal gambling and female prostitution activities together were another estimated $10 billion. To these sums should be added income from other organized illegal activities such as loan-sharking insurance payments for arson for profit (which in 1982 totaled an estimated $440 million) and excise taxes evaded on smuggled cigarettes (an estimated $337 million in 1977).

The amassing of substantial and largely untaxed wealth by the underworld is a phenomenon that has persisted since prohibition. Recent interest in the tax evasion and the role of the underground economy highlights untaxed wealth as a serious obstacle to the goal of tax equity. Underworld profits continue to grow despite special-emphasis programs, such as the accelerated use of electronic surveillances, interagency strike forces to attack both organized crime and drug trafficking, substantial increases in enforcement personnel,and innovative legal approaches to racketeering, such as the Racketeer Influenced and Corrupt Organizations (RICO) and the Continuing Criminal Enterprise (CCE) statutes.

Little is know about money generated in the illegal sector of the underground economy. Profit estimates are based on assumptions about market forces in the underworld, the dynamics of which are only just beginning to be understood.[2] Controversy continues over where federal efforts should be more realistically focused: the control and containment of organized crime activities or their reduction or elimination. Decision makers are divided over how enforcement strategies should be split between combating crime and retrieving profits because there are few reliable figures indicating whether any approach to combating organized crime or narcotics traffic over the last thirty years has been successful. Consequently it is important to examine some factors associated with the production of illegal wealth in order to understand why current efforts seem ineffective in retrieving it and to determine whether any available alternatives promise improvement.

In response to limited progress made in combating sophisticated crime, the federal Justice and Treasury enforcement agencies have shifted their focus toward retrieving the lucrative profits generated by illicit activities, emphasizing the billions of dollars involved in organized narcotics trafficking. They have designed a two-pronged campaign designed to capture the wealth generated by illegal activities. One aim is to remove the economic incentives of crime by stripping violators of the monetary and other tangible fruits of their activities. They reason that the loss of profits constitutes a financial deterrent to offenders whose primary motives are economic. The other aim is to trace wealth that cannot be accounted for from legitimate sources back to its origin, in the expectation that this exercise will lead to evidence of illegal activities that produced the income.

This dual-phase approach rests on two assumptions about what criminals do with their profits. The first is that criminals want to enjoy their wealth without arousing too much suspicion. Most profits earned in the illegal sector of the underground economy eventually should surface in the legitimate sector of the economy. To accomplish their objective, criminals need access to a process that offers one or more of these advantages: obscures the origin of the ill-gotten money, is persuasive in representing that the money's origin was purely legitimate, or thoroughly confounds efforts to make sense out of where the money came from, how much is involved, and where it was spent.

The second assumption addresses the destination of illegal earnings after they surface in the legitimate economy. Transactions that convert illegally earned money to legitimate financial instruments are often less difficult to reconstruct, if only marginally, than the well-planned conspiratorial crimes that generated the money. The difference between legitimate and illegitimate transactions, however, is often the audit trail, which, although carefully obscured, accompanies legitimate transactions but is characteristically absent from illegal transactions. Such trails usually consist of four basic types of records, the first of three of which are features of everyday financial and commercial transactions: paperbased negotiable instruments such as money orders and cashiers' checks; public documents that record such transactions as incorporation, sales, and lending; and archival records of such institutional nonpaper transactions as electronic funds transfer. The fourth element in an audit is completed Treasury Department forms, known as Currency Transaction Reports (CTRs), that record currency exchange, or Currency or Monetary Instrument Reports (CMIRs) that record currency export. These forms were initiated by the Treasury Department to create an audit trail at critical points where no such trails had existed previously.

The Phenomenon of Money Laundering

Money laundering is the process of converting quantities of cash—generally currency that has been tainted in some way—to a form that can be used more conveniently in commerce and ideally conceals the origin of converted funds. The term is used in common parlance to refer to a variety of different processes, all of which satisfy the basic criteria of putting illegally earned (or "dirty") money into a financial system where it is exchanged, or "laundered," by conversion into an instrument or other asset, from which it finally exits in a form that appears to be free from the original taint and is "clean."

The focus on appearance regarding the money's origin is central to the role that laundering plays in underworld finance because the more accurate the perception is of legal origin, the less likely it is that probing questions regarding origin will be asked. Even if such questions are asked, the laundering process causes extraordinary frustration for the people who attempt to trace assets. The result is that law enforcement inquiries are relatively rare events compared with the frequency of laundering transactions. Adroit use of laundering techniques has succeeded in frustrating modest federal efforts to date in employing these remedial tools.

To illustrate this point, 1981 federal currency and asset seizure and forfeiture actions, as well as narcotics-related Internal Revenue Service civil tax penalties and assessments, totaled $296 million.[3] Comparing the midpoints of other reputable estimates of 1981 narcotics proceeds ($45 billion) with government data on 1981 removal actions (those instituted in 1981 but probably involving income generated in several prior years), one concludes that $0.0062 out of every illegally earned dollar from narcotics traffic is subject to the initiation of some type of government removal action. This figure loses further significance when one looks at the outcomes of various removal actions: less than half the amounts involved in seizure and forfeiture actions were actually surrendered to the government, and no more than 2 percent of IRS jeopardy and termination assessments (which totaled $81.3 million in 1981) ended up being collected. In light of these statistics, the value of asset removal strategies is highly questionable.

Money laundering actually describes two distinct types of process. In its first and most limited sense, the term describes the conversion of cash by exchanging a volume of illegally earned currency for some type of negotiable instrument or other asset that can be used in commerce without revealing the illegal source of the funds used to purchase it. Criminals who employ this basic process usually hold on to the instrument until such time as they want to reconvert it to cash or surrender it for some other purpose. This mode of laundering appears to be popular with criminals at the lower levels of trafficking or organized crime organizations, who prefer to spend their earnings quickly and among neophytes to the trade who are unfamiliar with the constellation of investment opportunities available with a little expert financial advice.

In its second and more widely accepted usage, money laundering refers to a sequence of discrete steps that begin essentially where the currency conversion process leaves off. In this process, laundering is a method for acquiring an asset, or interest in an asset, so that the owner may both account for and enjoy wealth while remaining immune to successful probes into the tainted origin of that wealth. This more expansive view of laundering demonstrates the characteristic underworld preference for shrouding illegal activities in extraordinary levels of secrecy. In the case of laundering, this is usually accomplished by multiplying the number of financial transactions that are necessary to consummate a fairly simple sale or exchange, such as the purchase of real estate. In this way, it becomes difficult for investigators to reconstruct facts surrounding each laundering transaction and to move from that point toward the allegedly illegal origin of the funds in question. This is essentially the rationale for using complicated banking and, especially, offshore and foreign banking arrangements to conceal both the origin and ownership of assets.

According to anecdotal information, factors that help account for choices among laundering modes include personal consumption patterns, attitudes toward financial risk, and preferences for degrees of secrecy. Criminals at the lower levels of trafficking and organized crime groups frequently demonstrate a remarkable lack of sophistication in their choice of a particular laundering mode, a fact attested to by the relative ease of law enforcement detection and apprehension in these cases and the possibility that government (primarily U.S. Customs) enforcement efforts manage to catch substantial numbers of relatively insignificant or financially uneducated violators.

Lack of sophistication is most evident when criminals fail to take advantage of more involved laundering options that offer additional degrees of secrecy without compromising the income-producing potential of their assets. On this point, it is important to note that a proportion of criminals hide the existence of their illegal wealth simply by sitting on their cash earnings, thereby frustrating enforcement efforts to find either an audit trail or conspicuous spending that is unsupported by reports of legally earned income. While this behavior limits the vulnerability of these criminals to successful law enforcement probes, it also restricts their freedom to acquire assets as conspicuously as other criminals who make the effort to launder their profits. We do not know the extent of this anomaly but are reminded of the scores of older-generation Mafia and other underworld leaders whose passion for anonymity was so strong that few investigators claimed to know what actually happened to the profits of these leaders and their organizations.

The role of foreign and offshore banking in money laundering has taken center stage in most recent reviews of laundering activity.[4] Foreign banking secrecy probably will continue to frustrate the investigation of substantial numbers of laundering schemes, and no short-term remedy promises much of a change. The number of jurisdictions that continue (and clearly will continue) to offer blanket secrecy involving customers' transactions outnumber those, such as the Cayman Islands, that are relaxing certain restrictions in order to aid U.S. criminal investigations. For example, recent attention has focused on the increasing use of Panama as a tax haven by criminals because its laws offer benefits that are disappearing in some other tax haven countries. Despite the concerted efforts of the U.S. government to impose certain limitations on blanket secrecy provisions of many of these jurisdictions, several factors will continue to work against the important benefits that these changes offer. They include the shifting of laundering transactions to other friendly jurisdictions that still abound, procedural difficulties in piercing bank secrecy in enough cases to make a real difference in the amount of laundering that occurs, and the rarely discussed option criminals have of relying on U.S. banking institutions for more laundering volume than currently supported.

Money laundering has other connotations as well, depending on whether criminals desire to evade payment of an obligation, such as income taxes, that results from the production of income by their cleansed asset or use of legitimate source capital (such as corportate profits) for an illegal purpose (such as foreign commercial bribery). By increasing the number of the steps involved in laundering illegal funds, criminals try to obscure the origin of funds used to acquire assets. This renders it extremely difficult to make inferences about the presumed origin of those funds, at least with enough credibility to satisfy legal standards of proof. If a particular laundering transaction is questioned, which is increasingly the case, the use of multiple transactions preceding and following the one under scrutiny makes it difficult to confirm that the asset was obtained with funds that were other than legal in origin. As a general finding, it does not seem to make much difference whether enforcement agencies plan to attack laundering with either criminal or civil sanctions; frustration over tracing assets back to their illegal origin is often enough to hamstring the investigation at the threshold level of suspicion.

Laundering in Perspective

Law enforcement and national media attention have focused recently on the issue of money laundering, presenting it as a problem separate from narcotics and organized crime enforcement. Specifically current enforcement emphasis on money laundering has evolved not as a policy of primary choice but out of default; emphasis has been placed on laundering because of the inability to control or reduce illegitimate, profitable activities. In order to determine whether this enforcement method has a chance to succeed in the wake of problems with earlier approaches, it is important to place the money laundering phenomenon in perspective. Accordingly it may be helpful to review the relationship between the money laundering process and underworld factors that give rise to it.

Drug trafficking is estimated to produce anywhere from $22 billion to $89 billion in illegal wealth annually. The inability of law enforcement to prevent illegal crop cultivation, illicit drug manufacture, and smuggling contributes to this sum. The problem of channeling billions of illegally earned dollars into the United States would not be nearly so formidable were it not for the failure of both domestic and foreign enforcement activities to reduce opportunities for making illegal profits.

By default, therefore, an enforcement focus on money laundering represents something on the order of a fourth-level defensive strategy. It comes into play long after the first (cultivation), second (manufacture), and third (smuggling) intelligence and enforcement defenses have been ineffective. Consequently it may be unfair to expect that targeting an enforcement campaign on laundering activity will compensate for the continued failure of efforts to reduce the criminal activities that inexorably lead to laundering. So long as the markets that generate illegal wealth succeed in withstanding interruptions by enforcement agencies, the problem of laundering will remain.

At this point, we should examine the consequence of policy failures to control the flow of illegally earned wealth into legitimate financial sectors. Criminals who acquire assets with laundered funds share many of the same general financial objectives as law-abiding citizens. With respect to investments, there is every reason to believe that criminals seek a return on their legitimate investments that is consistent with factors of risk associated with the investment mode they have chosen. Other obvious commonly shared objectives include the use of laundered assets as equity that can leverage other legitimate transactions (and the more valuable the asset, the more it can leverage), the discretion to liquidate assets in order to apply the proceeds to any number of other financial options, the use of assets to benefit from tax incentives and shelters available to all investors, and the use of assets in a variety of income-producing capacities.

Underworld entrepreneurs share certain characteristics associated with economically motivate entrepreneurs in general. Perhaps the most obvious feature is the propensity to take extraordinary risks, particularly in new and different marketplaces, in order to generate substantial profits. What really distinguishes illegal entrepreneurs from their legitimate sector counterparts is the decision to market an illegal commodity or service that has been stigmatized by the law as harmful to society.

The relationship of criminal entrepreneurship to the issue of money laundering is important to clarify. It involves the implications of criminals' shifting their risk-to-return financial orientation from the illegal to the legal sector of the economy. By investing laundered funds in legitimate financial institutions, criminals subject themselves to certain restrictions on their freedom to manipulate legitmate assets in illegal ways. (Of course there are exceptions; the first that comes to mind is tax evasion.) Overall it could be argued that society stands to suffer relatively less harm from the investment of racketeering proceeds in sectors where financial transactions are expected to conform to certain basic standards that govern the uses to which those assets can be put. consequently criminals whose laundered funds come to reside in banking, real estate, and securities investment must sacrifice a degree of discretion to behave illegally with respect to those investments in order that they might preserve the illusion of propriety, which, after all, is largely responsible for laundering activity in the first place.

Although law enforcement officials argue that the discretion to act illegally can be documented in a variety of situations such as real estate and other investor fraud, a review of the process of laundering funds through investment in the legitimate sector turns up more pressures toward civility than impropriety, although the strength and resolution of those pressures is difficult to calculate. Considering the origin of most laundered funds and the goals of criminal entrepreneurs in taking antisocial risks to generate wealth, this may be a fortunate, if ironic, development for society. Overall, therefore, the investment of criminal proceeds in such ventures as construction of condominiums and purchases of shopping centers clearly involves a less—and probably far less—set of socially hazardous transactions than investment of those profits in additional illegal activities.

Some Potential Solutions

What improvements in current enforcement efforts to combat laundering would be made? It may be helpful to recall that only about 0.0062 percent of each dollar earned in drug trafficking is vulnerable to some form of asset retrieval, from outright seizure to more procedurally involved tax taking, by the federal government. Designing and implementing enforcement programs to improve this performance will be a formidable challenge. To this end, it may be instructive to examine the commitment of current resources, including personnel skill levels, organizational strategies, and legal and regulatory changes.

Banks and the Issue of Currency Reporting

U.S. banking institutions have been subjected to substantial criticism for being virtual aiders and abettors of laundering activity, apart from cases where bank employees and officers have been bribed to overlook laundering violations. Most of the criticism is directed at the uneven zeal shown by commercial banks in seeing that Treasury currency reporting forms (CTRs) are completed by their employees for each currency exchange transaction. After a number of prosecutions for noncompliance, especially in Florida and New York, Treasury officials report a marked improvement in compliance with the requirement for filling out and filing CTRs. However, fundamental detection problems associated with currency conversion as the first, and in many ways most important, step in the laundering sequence are sure to continue.[5]

Briefly, the following problems need to be addressed: (1) lack of emphasis on validating the identity of the party who is making the currency exchange, including couriers or traffickers with false identification documents; (2) bank discretion on when to exempt customers who exchange currency frequently from filing CTR reports, and this exemption favors any number of abuses—including currency exchanges that serve as laundries and attorneys whose deposit of cash in escrow accounts may serve as a laundering vehicle; (3) the ability to transfer funds by wire from bank to bank and country to country, making tracing of laundered assets next to impossible, especially since wire funds tranfers are exempt from CTR and other Treasury (CMIR) reporting requirements; (4) the ability of a number of financial institutions other than banks to act essentially as banks although they are exempt from currency reporting requirements, include gambling casinos and commodity exchanges (stock brokerage houses are responsible for filing CTRs, but their compliance rate is reportedly low); and (5) Treasury Department delays in entering CTRs into computers, thereby reducing whatever proactive potential CTRs inherently offer.

Innovative Law Enforcement Techniques

One of the first law enforcement innovations chosen to combat laundering was a variation of the sting approach. Undercover federal investigators posed as drug traffickers who wanted to launder substantial sums of money and enlisted the services of a number of bank personnel, financial advisers, and others in criminal violations associated with failure to comply with Treasury reporting requirements.

This variation of the sting approach offers substantial benefits as an enforcement strategy. First, it places investigators with the operations of financial institutions, an area about which investigators have little knowledge. This new knowledge of financial operations can be put to a number of constructive uses, not the least of which is to learn where in the workings of financial institutions crimes can be reconstructed, especially if one or more sources of information (such as paper documentation) is not available. Second, these so-called reverse undercover strategies tend to make experienced criminals wary of initiating new and potentially dangerous interactions.

Reports of the success of this strategy are mixed, but the approach would appear to offer the most potential impact where large numbers of entrepreneurs, new to a particular illegal activity, are forced by circumstance to enter into business relationships without having either the time or information resources to check into the parties with whom they are dealing. Therefore use of undercover personnel to assume the roles of drug traffickers, bankers, financial advisers, and others can be expected to produce large numbers of prosecutions that are requisite to meaningful deterrence and an increased reluctance on the part of experienced criminals to deal with neophytes.

Skill Development

The discussion so far underscores the value to enforcement personnel of on-the-job exposure to the workings of financial institutions that function in a laundering capacity. A separate and distinct problem is the need for all federal agencies that investigate narcotics, organized crime, tax, and currency violations to develop skills in the investigation of laundering. Currently there is no instructional, reference, or other educational material that explains either the general phenomenon of money laundering or its links to various financial institutions and other businesses engaged in this type of activity. The development of cadres of experienced personnel in south Florida, for example, has been of limited value because skilled personnel from the Internal Revenue Service, Drug Enforcement Administration, and the Customs Service were scattered to at least twelve other localities where the complexion of the underworld, local laundering preferences, and skill levels within their agencies differed substantially from the situation of critical mass that prevailed in south Florida. Consequently investigators who increasingly come upon new wrinkles in laundering techniques (such as commodity brokerage accounts) are provided with little guidance from their own agencies. Unless this situation improves drastically in the near future, difficulties encountered by investigators in trying to unravel laundering schemes will continue to impose artificial limitations on the use of both criminal and civil asset-retrieval tools.

Conclusion

Considering the ineffectiveness of current policies to combat money laundering, it may be difficult to invoke meaningful remedies. Reforms and innovations that appear to be feasible may result in a rise in the number of laundering-related prosecutions and asset removal actions. The sheer enormity of the problem, however, and the numbers of criminals involved in laundering activities and their laundering transactions would seem to call for a geometric increase in punitive actions, an unlikely event.

At least in the near term, laundering will endure as a process, however stigmatized, that facilitates the movement of criminal wealth from socially harmful origins to relatively more productive ends. After nearly six decades of notable failures in trying to reduce organized commerce in illegal goods and services, this state of affairs may pass for a policy otherwise described as negotiated order and implicit regulation. On balance, therefore, perhaps the lack of success that has plagued efforts to combat organized drug trafficking represents only a partial setback for the public good.

Notes

1. U.S. Treasury Department, Internal Revenue Service, *Income Tax Compliance Research: Estimates for 1973–1981* (Washington, D.C.: Internal Revenue Service, 1983), chaps. 1–4; and appendix G; National Narcotics Intelligence Consumers Committee (NNICC), *The Supply of Drugs to the U.S. Illicit Market from Foreign and Domestic Sources in 1981* (Washington, D.C.: Drug Enforcement Administration, 1982).

2. Most of the advances in this area are recorded in three publications: Carl Simon and Anne Witte, *Beating the System* (Cambridge, Mass.: Auburn House, 1982); Peter Reuter, *Disorganized Crime: The Economics of the Visible Hand* (Cambridge: MIT Press, 1983); and Jonathan Rubenstein and Peter Reuter, *Illegal Gambling in New York: A Case Study in the Operation, Structure, and Regulation of the Illegal Market* (Washington, D.C.: Government Printing Office, 1982).

3. These were totaled by combining the various seizure, forfeiture, and tax penalty statistics contained in the 1981 NNICC report, as well as the 1982 NNICC report.

4. U.S. Senate, Permanent Subcommittee on Investigations, *Crime and Secrecy: The Use of Offshore Banks and Companies* (Washington, D.C.: Government Printing Office, 1983); Richard H. Blum "Offshore Money Flows: A Large Dark Number" (unpublished manuscript, 1981); and U.S. House of Representatives, Committee on Government Operations, *Tax Evasion through the Netherlands Antilles and Other Tax Haven Countries* (Washington, D.C.: Government Printing Office, 1983).

5. U.S. House of Representatives, Subcommittee on General Oversight and Renegotiation, Committee on Banking, Finance, and Urban Affairs *Hearing, To Investigate the Enforcement and Effectiveness of the Bank Secrecy Act* (Washington, D.C.: Government Printing Office, 1982).

4
Racketeers as Cartel Organizers

Peter Reuter

T
he observation that criminal entrepreneurs often have major
holdings in legitimate enterprises is one that has always
caused great concern. Landesco (1929), in his landmark study
of organized crime in Chicago in the first quarter of this century,
commented on the numerous legitimate enterprises of the major
bootleggers. The Kefauver committee (1950), despite its emphasis
on illegal gambling, also drew up a list of fifty industries, ranging
from steel production to liquor distribution, in which it "found evidence of hoodlum infiltration." Indeed, given the rather crude labels
on the industries in the list, it was hard to identify industries that
were clearly excluded. The President's Commission on Law Enforcement and the Administration of Justice (1967:4) ominously warned
that "law enforcement officials agree that entry into legitimate business is continually increasing." Since 1967 the flow or reports of
such entry has continued.[1]

Why is racketeer investment in legitimate enterprises considered
a serious problem? One might argue that it represents a less threatening use of criminal energies and funds than further investment in
illegal markets. Surely we prefer narcotics dealers to spend more of
their time and money on ownership of real estate than selling drugs.

There are a number of responses. First, it is widely asumed that
racketeers bring to their legal interests the same techniques of corruption, intimidation, and fraud that they use in their illegal enterprises. In effect, they pollute legal markets.[2] Second, there is only a
slight diminution in the intensity of their illegal activities. Heroin
importers who invest in real estate do not, by so doing, pass up
significant opportunities in the heroin business. It may simply be

This chapter is drawn from an ongoing study of racketeering in legitimate industries.
The research was supported by grants from the National Institute of Justice. The
views expressed are solely the responsibility of the author and should not be identified
as those of the Rand Corporation or its sponsors.

difficult for them to expand through reinvestment in heroin without substantially increasing their risk.[3] Third, involvement in legal enterprises may actually assist the illegal enterprises. For example, bar ownership provides criminals with a protected yet public place to meet with their associates. It may also enable them to account for large volumes of small bills and coins accumulated in the numbers business, if so involved. Fourth, illegal entrepreneurs may be able to use their criminal assets to assist their legal enterprises and disadvantage their noncriminal counterparts. For example, a retail outlet that also provides customers access to some illegal goods and services will have an advantage over the outlets of competitors that provide only legal goods. The owner's reputation as a criminal entrepreneur, particularly where the buyers are not final customers, may enable him to attract business from buyers who are concerned to avoid criminal violence against them.

Although all these matters are worth investigating, attention here will be restricted to a subclass of legitimate markets in which racketeers are involved and seem to have acquired the power to influence the conduct of the market as a whole. What are the instruments or techniques by which racketeers acquire their power in the market?

Definitional Preliminaries

Here we are concerned with a specific subset of criminals. No doubt people who have made large sums through theft, fraud, and a variety of other crimes also invest in legitimate businesses. Anecdote suggests that they generally retire from the illegal business that generated the initial capital for their purchase of the legal enterprise, if only because much conventional criminal activity is best suited to young men. While we may deplore the ability of a criminal to live comfortably on his ill-gotten gains, it is not generally seen as a significant issue of public policy.

There is, however, a subclass of criminals that presents a very different problem; these are racketeers, persons who are members of a large group with a continuing identity, specified (though broadly defined) roles for individuals, and a range of criminal interests. The Mafia is one such group, but there are others, including motorcycle gangs. They present a different problem for government because it is assumed, with some credence, that they occasionally use the powers that arise from membership in the criminal group to support their investments in legitimate firms. Alternatively they may play an important role in extorting legitimate enterprises, even without investment.[4]

I use the term *racketeer* rather than *organized crime* only because it seems to have acquired fewer complicating secondary meanings. It is also the term that finds most currency in legal and political usage. Racketeer-Influenced and Corrupt Organizations (RICO) is the title of the federal statute that deals most nearly with this phenomenon. *Labor racketeering* is the universal term for a closely related activity, intrusion of members of criminal groups into positions of power within unions.

Nonetheless, it is difficult to find a satisfactory definition of *rackets*. Dictionary definitions are generally unhelpful, providing historical detail about the development of a term, which is usually regarded as colloquial.[5] Statutory definitions are unconvincing. The federal statutes define a racketeer as a person who is convicted of two felonies, drawn from a broad list, within ten years of each other. The list includes extortion, corruption, and the provision of a number of illegal goods and services (such as narcotics and gambling).[6] While this may define a class of offenders that should be dealt with particularly severely, it is not a convincing definition of racketeering.

An example may suggest the nature of the problem. Kwitny (1979) describes in great detail the role of an entrepreneur named Moe Steinman in the New York meat industry. Steinman had a close association with many Mafia members but himself had no criminal record prior to the episode that Kwitny describes. Indeed all of his activites seem to have been associated with the meat industry. He used his relations with the union leaders to extort the suppliers and buyers of meat. Each party was, individually though not corporately, paid out of the fruits of the extortion. For instance, purchasing officers for various supermarket chains received kickbacks in return for ignoring extortionate prices. Steinman's power was certainly based in part on his known connections with Mafia members, though the available information suggests that he made little use of mafiosi and directed them rather than vice-versa. Was Steinman a racketeer? He was certainly not a member of any criminal organization, except inasmuch as one wishes to use that term for the association (long-lasting but opportunistic and informal) that he had with Mafia members. That seems to stretch the term *member* much too far. Nonetheless, it would seem that racketeering is a reasonable description of his activities within the meat distribution industry of New York.

The Steinman example suggests serious definitional problems. Here is a case where, whatever the historical origins of Steinman's power, the activity is essentially internal to the market. Corporations and customers were extorted by a conspiracy of individuals who had well-defined legitimate roles within the industry. It might be seen as a form of white-collar crime, for the criminality did rest on the use of occupationally determined power, but the breadth of conspiracy and the determinedly blue-collar nature of many of the critical participants makes that a questionable classification. Perhaps the critical characteristic is the underlying threat of violence. Whatever Steinman's relationship with the Mafia, it is clear that he could ensure the use of violence, if not against individuals at least against property. This distinguishes his conspiracy from those conventionally attacked by antitrust.

Racketeers should be identified by their ability to invoke credible threats of violence against a broad array of persons and organizations. There is a distinction between this and the bully dependent on his own physical prowess. Racketeers must be believed to command an organization that can execute their threats in a way that permits them to avoid apprehension and to protect themselves against retaliation. Members of the Mafia clearly meet this requirement, though not all of them may be racketeers.

Racketeering is a particular activity on the part of racketeers; not everything that racketeers do is racketeering. It is the use of their reputation as racketeers to command the actions of others that constitutes racketeering. A Mafia member who engages in bookmaking is simply a bookmaker. A Mafia member who receives payments from other bookmakers in order to protect them, either from himself or from extortion by other criminals, is engaged in racketeering. Similarly a Mafia member who owns a bar is simply a bar owner. When he forces all bars to pay him in order to avoid labor difficulties or outbreaks of violence (which might lead to loss of license) in the bar, then he is racketeering.

Racketeers in the Legitimate Economy: a Classification

At least three factors may explain racketeer diversification into legitimate business investments. First, illegal enterprises have high legal and financial risks associated with them (see Reuter 1983). The rational criminal entrepreneur, as his wealth and income increase, will diversity so as to reduce the overall risks he faces. Second, it is, apparently, difficult to capitalize the profits of illegal enterprises. Briefly, the argument is that since the books are unauditable, there is, for example, not a ready market of buyers will to take over a numbers bank at a reasonable multiple of earnings. Moreover, the enterprise is a personal entity whose continued functioning is dependent on the ability of a new owner to retain the loyalty of participants in it. Hence, the racketeer, if he wishes to pass on wealth to his family, may choose to invest in other enterprises also. Third, investment in legitimate businesses not only helps deal with tax authorities but also provides a patina of respectability, which may be of increasing importance to the aging racketeer.[7]

None of these factors suggests that the racketeer's investment will threaten the integrity of a legitimate market. And indeed there may be many racketeer investments of a relatively passive nature. While the focus here is on industries in which they appear to play an active role, there is no suggestion that this is a complete description of their role in the legitimate economy. There appear to be numerous instances in which racketeers acquire control of small stores and businesses and permit the existing management to continue.[8]

For policy purposes, racketeer involvement in legitimate enterprises may be arrayed on a spectrum of seriousness. If one end of the spectrum of activities covered by the term *racketeer infiltration of legitimate business* (the term most commonly used in policy and legal discussions) is represented by passive investments, the midpoint is given by those businesses that are complementary to the rackets. Bars represent an attractive investment to racketeers, at least in part, because the bars can be used as outlets for illegal services and meeting places for the racketeer and his associates. The bar may be operated as it was prior to the racketeer's investments. The racketeer may skim no higher percentage of revenues than the average bar owner and may not interfere with local competitors. For law enforcement it is not the operation of the bar itself that represents the problem; it is the use of the bar as a component of the illegal enterprises of the racketeer.

More serious is the opportunistic and short-term investment in a single legitimate business that is used to defraud other businesses. Kwitny (1979) provides many interesting examples of this. The firm typically is used to generate cash through conventional short-term credit arrangements. The racketeer, whose involvement in the enterprise is effectively concealed, removes the assets of the firm, including this short-term credit, leaving behind a bankrupt corporation and a sufficiently tangled skein of paper that law enforcement and tax agencies are unable to convict him.

The most serious form of racketeer involvement in the legitimate economy is racketeer control of a market industry. It is clear that racketeers had enormous influence over the garment industry of New York during the 1930s (Block 1980). No history of that industry is complete without a discussion of the racketeer's involvement in labor-management disputes and extortion of individual corporations. Similar allegations have been made about other industries over the decades, from liquor wholesaling to meatpacking.

Most of these studies of racket-controlled industries have been concerned with describing incidents of racketeering (Seidman 1942), while scholarly literature generally has ignored altogether their involvement in the legitimate economy. Ianni (1972) is an exception, but his analysis of the Lupollo family focuses on their internal relations rather than the consequences of their involvement in legal enterprises. Anderson (1979) provides a detailed analysis of the legitimate business interests of a Mafia family in an unidentified city, but she asserts that there is no evidence that the family controls any legitimate industry in the city. Studies of labor racketeering have been essentially historical, concerned with the consequences of abuse of power for the unions, not the industries in which they operated. Hutchinson (1972) provides the richest account of the history of labor racketeering, drawing almost entirely on published materials, particularly the various hearings of the McClellan committee.[9] Neither Hutchison nor Taft (1958), in his lectures on labor racketeering, provides an analytic framework in which to consider the historical record and answer the two central questions: Why is racketeering an endemic problem in some unions and industries, and not in others? What are the consequences of racketeering to these unions and industries?

Perhaps the most interesting study of racketeer involvement in the legitimate economy is that of Block (1980), dealing with New York in the period 1920–1950. In particular, Block considers a number of industries in which racketeers, predominantly Jewish, played a significant role. In most cases that role arose from labor problems. Management and/or labor brought in a group of racketeers to defend their interests in the course of struggles over unionization. The racketeers in some cases came to control the union and occasionally were instrumental in forming employer associations. These associations had the dual function of dealing more effectively with the unions and suppressing competition during periods (particularly in the depression) when many firms were at the margin of bankruptcy.

Block tries to explain why in some industries the racketeering was limited only to abuse of labor power. He notes, for example, that racketeering in the restaurant industry never went beyond the signing of sweetheart contracts, though an employers' association was formed.

> The point here is that even in cases where businessmen may not have been instrumental in establishing rackets they would cooperate with extortionists as long as they could control the labor market. Without oligopolistic tendencies within the industry, there was no necessity for a trade association which was in this case a pure extortion front, unlike the trade associations in the needle trades. (p. 197)

In the fur trades, on the other hand, the racketeers' sole involvement was in the creation and maintenance of an employers' association designed to suppress competition (Block 1980:173–176).

Racketeer Domination: Instruments

How may a whole industry be brought under the control of racketeers? No doubt there are various methods that have been used in twentieth-century American business history; however anecdote, the legal record, newspaper reports, and congressional hearings all suggest that corrupt labor unions have played an important, probably dominant, role in such racketeering. Control of an essential factor confers the power to extort. Antitrust serves as a constraint on efforts to dominate any input to a market except one—labor. Control of a union, which is automatically exempted from antitrust, offers a unique opportunity for extortion of an industry.[10]

This is not to deny that racketeers enter the legitimate economy by other means. The gambling debt of a store owner, the financial problems of a garment manufacturer, a racketeer's willingness to pay more than the market price for a restaurant or bar: any of these may lead to a racketeer's acquiring control of a legitimate firm and using it as he wants. But the transition from individual enterprise to control over an entire market requires something more than a series of such opportunities.

This point is sufficiently important to be considered in more detail. In theory, racketeers could acquire control through unfair competition. Consider the racketeer who has ready access to a supply of untaxed cigarettes and stolen liquor. By offering lower prices in bars that he controls, the racketeer could drive out competitors and acquire control of the market. There are at least three objections to this theory. First, by concentrating the distribution of stolen goods through his own outlets, the racketeer raises the period during which he is at risk. Second, he provides an incentive to his competitors in the bar market to inform against him concerning his fencing activities. Finally, the takeover may be a lengthy process and there are numerous reasons for expecting that racketeers have short planning horizons.[11]

Another alternative is pure intimidation. Racketeers have a reputation for being able to execute threats of violence (indeed that is their defining attribute) and to suppress the course of justice when complaints are brought against them. A racketeer may choose to bully entrepreneurs into surrendering their autonomy. He may use a firm that he controls to buy out the competitors or to ensure that they coordinate their actions with his firm so as to maximize its revenues.

But there are problems with this approach. Not all entrepreneurs are likely to be susceptible to such bullying. The cost of a complaint may be very high if in fact racketeer control of law enforcement is imperfect. Newspaper campaigns may circumvent such control. While the strategy may have been adopted in some instances, there are no accounts of pure intimidation-based monopolies.[12] It is a high-risk strategy compared to the abuse of union power, through which bullying can be given an ideological twist.

How do unions provide the racketeer with means for organizing an employer conspiracy? The union is a perfect tool for disciplining firms that will not follow conspiracy rules, for it dresses up cartel enforcement as the more socially acceptable enforcement of union rules. Employers may find themselves hauled before grievance proceedings to face false charges of failure to meet their union obligations. Customers may find themselves picketed by workers claiming that the supplier is not properly unionized. If the employer is not already unionized, the union may refuse to permit unionization without the firm's also joining the conspiracy.

Obviously not all unions offer the same opportunities. The nature of the membership and the employers plays an important role. Unions with low-skill workers, who are less aware of their rights and perhaps less competent at exercising them, provide the best targets. Similarly industries consisting of numerous small firms selling essentially identical goods, using the same technology, are particularly vulnerable to labor racketeering. First, each firm is more seriously affected by a strike because of the ready availability of alternative suppliers. Their capital reserves may be more quickly exhausted also. Second, to the extent that the racketeer is able to guarantee to each firm that the same extortionate settlement is being applied industry-wide, the individual firm is less concerned that acceptance of the settlement will affect its competitive position (Schelling 1967).[13] Published materials on labor racketeering confirm these general hypotheses. It is in the fresh produce, garment trucking, and garbage collection markets, all characterized by small enterprises and low-skill labor, in which racketeers, through their union powers, have acquired their greatest control.[14]

Racketeer Domination: Goals and Constraints

So far the argument has concerned the instrument of control. Unions can offer a unique means for racketeer control of an industry. But what is the optimal strategy for racketeers who have the means to control an industry (whether through a union or some other tool) to exert that control?

One obvious method is intimidation on behalf of a single firm. Racketeers may choose to intimidate existing and potential competition of some firm they control, either through direct or hidden ownership. In the latter case, payments may be made to the racketeers from receipts that are not recorded by the entrepreneur (as is possible in many low level distributive trades where receipts are primarily cash) or through payments to consultants, who are themselves racketeers. For example, the late Carlo Gambino, reputedly the leading Mafia member during the 1960s and early 1970s, apparently owned a firm called SGS Associates, which claimed to offer labor consulting services.[15] Payments to the firm presumably were payments for racketeering services. Such services may have included intimidation of potential and actual rivals.

Such intimidation need be little more than a declaration of interest. SGS Associates was known, at least after McClellan committee hearings, to represent racketeering interests. The knowledge that SGS worked for some firms in a particular industry may have been sufficient to deter others from entering the industry. Indeed the sensible investor contemplating making such an entry might well have thought it prudent to approach SGS to determine what its attitude would be to another firm in the same industry. SGS might have been willing to offer similar services to the new entrant; certainly a statement that they would be unwilling to provide the services served as a warning to the entrant.

The incentive for intimidation of competition is obvious. The profits available from a particular industry are maximized when there is an effective monopoly. The racketeer, given his peculiar assets, should be able to reap most of the returns from conferring monopoly power on a particular firm.[16] However, there is significant risk associated with this strategy. A monopoly is particularly prone to come to the attention of antitrust authorities, even without information provided by aggrieved former competitors. Monopoly is a violation and presents the easiest target for antitrust authorities.[17] Intimidated businessmen may well go to law enforcement agencies, even when faced by threats by racketeers, since, unlike the criminals whom racketeers more commonly intimidate, they have little to fear from those agencies. Moreover, given that monopoly cases do not generally require testimony concerning conduct, the former competitors need not take the risk of exposing themselves by testifying in court.

At least two caveats ought to be raised. First, federal antitrust authority is restricted to activities that involve interstate commerce. While the courts have upheld very broad interpretations of the commerce clause, there do remain sectors of business that are treated as intrastate. In particular, much small business activity traditionally has been held to lie outside the reach of the federal laws in this respect. Indeed the first federal antitrust case against the garbage collection (carting) industry was contested on precisely those grounds.[18]

Until recently state antitrust enforcement has been weak. Some states lacked any specific antitrust statutes. Where there were statutes, there was often no specialized unit for their enforcement. In recent years there have been positive developments in both law and policy. A number of states have created antitrust codes where there were none, and others have strengthened existing statutes. With financial encouragement from the federal government, there has also been a development of antitrust sections within the offices of state attorneys general. While that may have some importance in the future, in looking at the recent historical record, there has been little or no antitrust activity (except for private suits) in many of the small business sectors where racketeers are likely to be influential. This lack of effective antitrust surveillance may have had some influence on the sectoral choice of racketeers, at least with respect to efforts to monopolize.

There is a second caveat to the argument claiming risk in monopolization. Monopoly can be disguised. The one company can have many names, with effective ownership disguised through a series of dummy corporations.[19] Such disguises are unlikely to prevent a determined investigation, but they may delay its advent and success. The monopoly does not have to be perpetual to be worth its cultivation.

Nonetheless, it is clear that there are certain legal risks arising from racketeer efforts to create monopoly through intimidation, even where that intimidation is dressed up as something else. There is an alternative method that reduces these risks and may yield similar benefits: racketeer instigation and taxation of an industry-wide cartel.[20] The members of the cartel might include all existing firms or only a large subgroup; that is a strategy decision that depends on perceived risks, such as the probability of nonmember complaint or aggressive nonmarket expansion.

The advantage of the cartel or conspiracy, especially if it includes all existing firms, is that there is little need for forceful intimidation. Firms must be persuaded to join the conspiracy, it is true, and that may involve the use of coercion. But coercion whose objective is to persuade an entrepreneur to join with colleagues in an arrangement that may, at least in the short run, increase his income is likely to be less disturbing than coercion whose objective is the elimination of an enterprise. Moreover, the conspiracy can be created without any disruption of customer relationships. Where the monopolist must move aggressively to take customers from rivals and then incur the disapprobation of sharp price increases once the rival is driven out, the cartel may leave each customer with his existing supplier. A cartel is less noticeable.

What does the racketeer bring to cartels? First, he may provide the initiating spirit. Not all entrepreneurs have the same willingness to enter into illegal arrangements. Racketeers, whose primary skills relate to criminal activities, presumably are more willing than business people generally to initiate illegal conspiracies. Further, entrepreneurs may be more willing to attend meetings for the purpose of hatching such agreements when the invitation is issued by a threatening figure.

More important, racketeers offer the prospect that the conspiracy will work, simply because of more effective enforcement of the rules. Many cartels appear to have a short life because there is always an incentive for a member to leave the conspiracy and take advantage of the restrictions that the group provides for the remaining members (Scherer 1970). If a cartel raises prices to the monopoly level, an entrepreneur can maximize his income by leaving the group pricing just below the conspiracy price. Potential conspirators are presumably aware of this. Hence they may be reluctant to enter into an agreement that is likely to be short-lived as well as illegal. Racketeers, by promising to take illegal but effective actions against any member who tries to break the rules of the conspiracy, provide potential members with credible assurance that it is likely to be of lasting benefit. Racketeers can then provide a number of critical services for conspiracies. They can bring the members together for the initial discussion, provide them with greater assurance that the conspiracy will last, and make it last by enforcing the rules.

Still another factor encourages cartel organization rather than monopoly franchising by racketeers. The analysis has assumed so far that there is a single racketeer interest. In fact, there are numerous racketeers, and they are clustered in a number of groups. Even within one group there may be competing interests with respect to a specific industry; various members may have involvements in different firms.[21] The strategy adopted by one racketeer to further the interests of his client may conflict with that of another racketeer. This potentially complicates the situation a great deal and may thus influence the choice of cartel rather than monopoly franchising.

It is necessary at this stage to make some statements about the relationships between the Mafia, apparently the most significant group of racketeers, and other groups and also about the relationships among members of the Mafia. It appears that there are various other criminal groups, generally ethnically homogeneous, that are either loosely affiliated with the Mafia or entirely independent of it. The Mafia may have a greater reputation for control of violent forces, but within particular communities some other group may be able to mount similarly powerful forces and have an equally violent reputation. Non-Mafia groups probably defer to the Mafia outside their host communities, but the relationship may be reversed within those communities. How well worked out are the relationships among the groups, at points of potential conflict, is impossible to say in a general fashion. We certainly have to allow for the possibility that the interests of different racketeering groups may be in conflict and that the conflict is not subject to any well-worked-out dispute resolution mechanism.

Even within the Mafia, it is unclear that competing interests are easily brought together. The traditional concept of the Mafia is that it is a highly centralized organization where the higher-level figures have command relationships with lower-level members. In this view, lower-level members must provide their bosses with information about their economic activities and even pay some taxes on these activities. However, there is a good deal of evidence and argument that contradicts. Mafia families may better be viewed as loose coalitions of smaller gangs that maintain a wary relationship with each other (Zeiger 1975). Gang boundaries may be defined territorially or functionally but are often unclear. Even within the gang, exchange of information may be quite limited, in response both to a concern about internal informants and about the lack of well-specified property rights. The more information a member provides about his own activities, the higher the probability that a higher-level member can extract the full tax and that other members can make raids on the customers and/or employees of his operations. This may be a function of changes in the Mafia and the environment in which it operates; the Americanization of the Mafia, with the collapse of family loyalty, may have reduced its cohesion.[22]

Racketeering interests in an industry are not necessarily unified. Racketeers, even within the same general group, may have competing interests that are difficult to resolve. It would also be a mistake to assume that racketeers do not face some of the same problems of resolving members' conflicts that other groups face. The leader may propose a solution that maximizes everyone's income, if only side payments are made. The more difficult task presumably is to persuade the competing members that it is in fact the preferred solution and to ensure that the side payments actually will be made.

It might be more sensible to assume that agreements are reached that maximize the revenues of both interests, subject to the constraint that no side payments be made. Where interests conflict, there may be an agreement in which both sides make concessions, but the concessions do not include the possibility of future payments by one party to compensate the other. The argument for assuming this restriction is the high level of mistrust that criminals are likely to have of each other, the lack of court-enforceable agreements, the relatively short planning horizons of criminal entrepreneurs (subject to the risk of imprisonment and homicide), and the ambiguity of verbal agreements.

Although special attention to the Mafia because of its reputation gives it potentially a distinctively important role in racketeering, there are many other criminal groups with some of the same attributes of coherent force, broad-based criminality, and hierarchical structure. In illegal markets, they may provide potent competition to the Mafia; however, their relative youth as organizations ensures that they have a less well-developed reputation in the community at large. The constant reporting of Mafia activities and the identification of individual members in headline stories permit them and their associates to intimidate noncriminals more easily than other racketeers.

This is not to say that another group of criminals could not organize a conspiracy of entrepreneurs in a particular community. But the group's reputational base is likely to be much narrower. It may be required to invest in actual use of violence, which has significant risk associated with it, in order to persuade potential conspirators that they will be able to enforce the rules. Further, it is unlikely that a group of entrepreneurs would actually invite them to organize the conspiracy, precisely because their reputation is less well established.[23]

In fact, there are a few accounts of non-Mafia racketeering groups taking control of an industry. Most of these come from an earlier era when there were other groups with equally well-established reputations. The predominantly Jewish groups in New York, associated with Arnold Rothstein, Louis Buchalter, and Jacob Shapiro, had broad-based reputations during the 1920s and 1930s. More recently there have been some claims of similar racketeering by predominantly Hispanic groups in southern California.

Conclusion

Given the sparseness of information concerning racketeer-controlled industries, any analysis must be highly speculative. The argument has been simply that there are constraints to the use of power by racketeers and that pure coercion is not likely to be a common path to industry dominance. Union corruption may be a prerequisite for effective control. Certainly unions provide a uniquely protected instrument for control. Once that control is attained, it may be optimal for racketeers to share the returns from this control through formation of a cartel rather than attempting to acquire full monopoly rents by franchising a monopolist and coercing all competitors from the market. This, in turn, makes the task of law enforcement agencies more difficult.

Notes

1. See, for example, Pennsylvania State Crime Commission (1980).
2. Anderson (1979) makes a similar argument. Her own data provided little support for it.
3. Formally, marginal rates of return to investments of capital and/or labor may be sharply declining.
4. Compare Anderson (1979:76).
5. The most useful is that of *Webster's New International Dictionary:*

"Racket: a usually illegitimate enterprise or activity that is made workable by coercion, bribery or intimidation . . . a system of obtaining money or other advantage illegally, fraudulently or undeservedly, usually with the outward consent of the victim." The same dictionary also provides a useful and distinctive definition of racketeer: "one who extorts money or advantage by threats of violence or by blackmail or by threatened or actual unlawful interference with business or employment."

6. The basis for the inclusion of gambling and narcotics is the explicit assumption of Congress that these are provided by organizations that can only flourish where they are able to corrupt law enforcement and/or intimidate potential competition.

7. A racketeer will seek to report sufficient income to avoid a net worth case, where the IRS shows that his visible increase in assets over a certain period is inconsistent with his reported income. Thus, for example, Angelo Bruno, the deceased Philadelphia Mafia leader, reported income from his association with John's Vending, though he apparently did little for the company.

8. Anderson (1979) reports numerous such instances with reservations about the completeness of her information.

9. "McClellan committee" is a shortened reference to the Permanent Subcommittee on Investigations of the Senate Committee on Government Operations, which was chaired by the late Senator John McClellan for two decades. Over a fifteen-year period, starting in 1956, the subcommittee held numerous hearings into the activities of organized crime, from labor racketeering to narcotics distribution.

10. The exemption is limited to its activities as a union. It has no such exemption, for example, in its investment activites.

11. Racketeers have a lower life expectancy than their legal counterparts and have considerable uncertainty about the period of time during which they will be able to operate without restriction (remain unincarcerated). Both factors raise the rate at which racketeers discount future returns.

12. The newspaper wars in Chicago and Philadelphia in the early part of this century might provide an exception if there had been a clear winner.

13. Extortionate refers not to the level of wage payments reached in the settlement but to the side payments demanded by the racketeers. These payments may be direct or may take the form of excessive prices for essential inputs to be pruchased from racketeer-controlled firms. Restaurant owners might, for example, be forced to pay excessive prices for purchase of linens in return for a lower wage contract for bartenders.

14. In order to permit more serious testing of these statements about the union and industrial settings in which labor racketeering is a problem, an effort was made to collect data on the incidence of labor racketeering held by an agency within the U.S. Department of Labor. Despite considerable assistance by many persons within the Department of Labor and the National Institute of Justice, legal obstacles finally prevented access to the data. Reuter (1981) provides a description of the effort, which may be of

some interest for those contemplating data collection from agencies in this field. The statements about past findings concerning the distribution of labor racketeering across industries are based on the McClellan committee hearings as summarized in Hutchison (1970).

15. On SGS, see *New York Times*, April 17, 1965. It was disbanded shortly after the *Times* article appeared, but at least one of Gambino's partners continued to offer the same service. There is some reason to believe that customers sought his services precisely because they believed SGS had not been disbanded.

16. There is a possible problem for the racketeer arising from the effective ownership of the business. In order to extort all the available profits, he must be able to determine what those profits are. While the racketeer is in a better position than tax authorities to get access to books and records, it is not a particularly demanding task for an entrepreneur to conceal income from a racketeer extortionist. Block (1980:chap. 7) provides some examples of frictions that arose from racketeers concerned that entrepreneurs were effectively concealing income from them.

17. The government need only prove the existence of a monopoly, usually defined as more than 65 percent of the market, to get a favorable ruling from the court. The trial usually centers on defining the market; the defense will argue for as broadly defined a market as possible, and the government will try to narrow the definition of the relevant market.

18. The case involving gargage collectors in Philadelphia can be found as case 1763 in Commerce Clearing House, *Trade Regulation Reports*, 1962.

19. Indeed, in the course of studying the solid waste industry, it was found that in one city with apparently a moderate level of concentration, the four largest firms operated out of one office.

20. Cartels can yield the full monopoly profits where there are no economies of scale beyond the size of the smallest cartel member.

21. The term *involvement* includes not only direct pecuniary investment but also patronage or kinship ties with the entrepreneur.

22. For a fuller statement of this view, see Reuter (1983:chap. 8). The most recent major Mafia informant, James Fratianno, asserts that values are changing within the families.

23. Block (1980), in his account of the fur trades, makes it clear that members of the industry sought out racketeers for just this purpose.

References

Anderson, Annelise. 1979. *The Business of Organized Crime*. Stanford, Calif.: Hoover Institution Press.

Block, Alan. 1980. *East Side-West Side: Organizing Crime in New York, 1930–1950*. Cardiff, Wales: University College, Cardiff Press.

De Maris, Ovid. 1981. *The Last Mafioso*. New York: Bantam Books.

Hutchison, John. 1972. *The Imperfect Union*. New York: E.P. Dutton.

Ianni, Francis A.J.A. 1972. *A Family Business: Kinship and Social Control in Organized Crime.* New York: Russell Sage Foundation.

Kwitny, Johathan. 1979. *Vicious Circles.* New York: W.W. Norton and Co.

Landesco, John. 1929. *Organized Crime in Chicago.* Chicago: University of Chicago Press; reissued, 1968.

Pennsylvania Crime Commission. 1980. *1980 Report: A Decade of Organized Crime.* St. Davids, Penn.

President's Commission on Law Enforcement and the Administration of Justice. 1967. *Task Force Report: Organized Crime.* Washington, D.C.: Government Printing Office.

Reuter, Peter. 1981. "Racketeering in Legitimate Industries." unpublished manuscript. Washington, D.C.: Rand Corporation.

———. 1983. *Disorganized Crime: The Economics of the Visible Hand.* Cambridge: MIT Press.

Schelling, Thomas. 1967. "Economic Analysis of Organized Crime." In President's Commission on Law Enforcement and the Administration of Justice *Task Force Report: Organized Crime.* Washington, D.C.: Government Printing Office.

Scherer, Frederick M. 1979. *Industrial Market Structure and Economic Performance.* Chicago: Rand McNally.

Seidman, Joel. 1942. *The Needle Trades.* New York: Farrar and Reinhart.

Taft, Phillip. 1958. *Corruption and Racketeering in the Labor Movement.* Ithaca: New York State School of Industrial and Labor Relations.

U.S. Congress. Senate. Special Committee to Investigate Organized Crime in Interstate Commerce (Kefauver committee). 1950–1951. *Hearings.* 19 parts in 19 volumes. *Reports* 4 parts in 1 volume. Washington, D.C.: Government Printing Office.

———. Select Committee on Improper Activities in the Labor or Management Field (McClellan committee). 1957–1968. *Hearings.* Washington, D.C.: Government Printing Office.

Zeiger, Henry. 1975. *The Jersey Mob.* Bergenfield, N.J.: New American Library.

5
Drug Enforcement and Organized Crime

Mark Kleiman

Organized crime—whether that phrase is restricted to its traditional sense as meaning the Mafia (La Cosa Nostra) or expanded to cover such emerging groups as motorcycle gangs—derives substantial revenue from drug trafficking. One objective of drug enforcement is to combat existing organized crime groups and to prevent or retard the emergence of new groups with the capacities, practices, and longevity that make organized crime a threat. Because a major effect of drug enforcement, and particularly of drug enforcement directed at importation and high-level domestic distribution, is to raise the price of drugs, and since the prices paid for drugs are the revenues of drug trafficking organizations, successful enforcement efforts may have the unintended effect of increasing the opportunities available to organized crime groups. Moreover, increased enforcement pressure may give competitive advantages to the most dangerous—most organized-crime-like—drug trafficking organizations at the expense of drug dealers less ready to employ violence and corruption. By contrast, retail level drug enforcement will be less prone to such unwanted side effects, and efforts to decrease consumer demand for illicit drugs will tend to reduce the revenues available to organized crime.

Drug traffickers commit a wide variety of crimes in addition to violations of the drug laws: tax evasion, bribery, obstruction of justice in all its forms, and all the degrees of assault and bodily harm including homicide (directed at each other, at officials, and at potential witnesses). Because they tend to have large amounts of portable wealth in the form of cash and drugs and because they cannot call for official help when threatened, they are also attractive targets for robbery and extortion, both for each other and for nondrug criminals, sometimes including police.

The crimes incident to drug trafficking (above the background level of crimes by and against businesses in general) are entirely artifacts of enforcement. Drug trafficking is forbidden not because the transactions themselves work harm but because drug sale facilitates and encourages drug consumption. The purpose of the drug laws is to suppress drug consumption and its attendant evils rather than the commercial activity as such. In this respect, the drug laws contrast with laws on prostitution where the commercial transaction is held to be a far greater evil than the underlying activity as a threat to both public morals and to the well-being of the prostitutes.

In evaluating the effects of various drug enforcement strategies on trafficking-related criminal activity, the drug law violations of drug possession, manufacture, and sale should be subordinated to nondrug crimes and on the acquisition of illicit incomes. From this perspective, the drug laws as a whole are always a losing proposition since they create crimes where none would otherwise exist. Nonetheless, it is not obvious whether the level of such crimes increases or decreases as controls become tighter and enforcement more rigorous from any starting point other than unregulated availability. Here the likely effects of variations in drug enforcement and other official drug abuse control strategies on the nature and extent of the organized crime problem are considered. As a preliminary, the effects of enforcement policy on the whole range of crimes by and against drug traffickers are examined.

Trafficking-Related Crimes

One can divide the predatory crimes associated with drug trafficking into two broad categories: (1) crimes among traffickers, and between traffickers and civilians or traffickers and police, generated by traffickers' attempts to avoid arrest and prosecution, and (2) crimes among traffickers as part of business disputes and acquisitive crime (robbery and extortion) directed against traffickers because of their inability to seek police protection. As shorthand, these might be called, respectively, enforcement violence and business violence. For evaluative purposes, we can think of alternative drug enforcement policies as determining the levels of these two kinds of trafficking-related crime, as well as the levels of drug consumption and user-related crime. In addition, drug strategy actions and outcomes can be arrayed along at least three other dimensions.

First, the effects can be immediate or long run, and the long run impact may differ in sign as well as in magnitude from the immediate effect. There are two different long runs in drug policy analysis. The long run of comparative statics—the equilibrium position after all actors have optimized their behavior under new conditions and the markets have had a chance to settle down—is different from historical-sociological long run in which actions form opinions and customs form tastes.

Second, the level of the traffic at which enforcement is directed can be differentiated. The conventional distinctions here are among source control, interdiction, distribution (or high-level domestic trafficking), wholesaling (or middle-level dealing), and street sales (low-level or retail dealing).

Third, the kind of drug involved differs. Here the conventional breakdown is into opiates (chiefly heroin), cannabis (chiefly marijuana), cocaine, hallucinogens (LSD, PCP), and various pharmaceutical synthetics, generically called "pills" and subdivided into stimulants (primarily various amphetamines), barbiturates, and other sedative-hypnotics (notably methaqualone). Different drugs have different effects on ancillary crime because of their pharmacology, the sociology of their consumption, and the technology and economics of their production and distribution. Enforcement actions at different levels of the traffic will have different effects on drug prices, other conditions of availability, and trafficking-related ancillary crime.

But from the perspective of citizens, legislators, and governmental chief executives, choices about, for example, the level of cocaine wholesaling investigations may not be within reach. Budgetary decisions are more commonly made in terms of totals available for drug investigation (at the state and local levels, sometimes even totals available for police work generally). The allocation of these resources across drugs and trafficking levels is then determined by investigative agency practices, agent incentives, and targets of opportunity. Thus it is useful to inquire about the effects of across-the-board changes in the resources available for drug enforcement, as well as asking more detailed questions about more finely targeted decisions.

Price Elasticity of Drug Demand

The key unknown in this analysis is the response of drug purchasers to increasing drug prices. If demand is relatively elastic to price—that is, if a given percentage price increase causes a more-than-proportionate percentage decrease in the quantity consumed—then increasing prices will lead to a decrease in the total amount of money spent on drugs, which means that the total revenues of drug trafficking organizations as a group will decrease. If, on the other hand, demand is relatively insensitive to price—if the price elasticity of demand is less than 1—then total drug-dealing revenues will increase as better enforcement drives prices up.

Heroin demand is likely to be rather inelastic in the short run because of the habitual nature of heavy heroin use. As is true of most other goods, heroin's long-run price elasticity is likely to be greater than its short-run elasticity because of turnover in the user population, because new users will tend to be more price sensitive than current users, and because a long spell of high prices is likely to cause some current users to make major life-style adjustments in the direction of reduced heroin use—for example, by entering treatment programs—that a temporary increase in price will not induce.

Even the most committed users will have to cut back on heroin purchases if the price rises to the point where, using all of their sources of income to the fullest and cutting all of their other expenditures to the bone, they are unable to afford their target level of the drug. Even if the increasing relative expense of heroin compared with alternative purchases does not cause them to choose to forgo some heroin consumption in favor of other pleasures, its increasing absolute expense pressing against available income will, by making them user effectively poorer, force cutbacks in all budget items, including heroin. (This is the income effect, as distinguished from the substitution effect, of increasing prices.) Thus the price elasticity of overall demand for drugs will depend partly on the share of total consumption accounted for by users whose drug expenditures loom very large in their budgets. This is probably true of most heroin addicts, and addicts probably consume the bulk of total heroin consumed, though they may be a minority of total users.

The same heavily skewed distribution of consumption is probably true of cocaine and marijuana consumers. Possibly only 20 percent of any group accounts for 80 percent of any activity. Take marijuana as an example. If there are 20 million users and consumption is 5,000 metric tons per year (Polich et al. 1984:42), then the average user smokes nearly two joints a day, enough to keep the person high for several hours.[1] Thus the average user must be very different from the typical user, since no such population of 20 million hard-core potheads is seen to exist. It seems far more plausible that a few million very heavy users stay stoned nearly all the time.

But even for these users, marijuana is unlikely to be such a dominant budget item that a moderate price increase would have major income effects. If 4 million (20 percent) of those users consumed 4,000 tons of marijuana (80 percent of the total) and if their purchases were made at wholesale prices, they would spend an average of about $1,000 per year on marijuana.

The substitution effects of marijuana price increases are also likely to be slight. With the cost of getting high on marijuana well under one dollar, the nonfinancial considerations must dominate most users' decisions about how often to use the substance, and the effects of moderate changes in price should be negligible. Thus marijuana should be inelastically demanded, even in the long run, and price increases due to better enforcement will raise traffickers' revenues.

The cocaine market is harder to discern. Cocaine is an expensive habit; the estimated 5 million cocaine users spend an average of about $1,500 per year on the drug (Reuter 1983b:17), and mechanically applying the 80/20 rule would lead one to imagine a million of the heaviest users averaging $6,000 per year each. This sort of luxury goods market has all sorts of cross-currents. The price is high compared with substitute goods and with normal incomes, but heavy users seem to be wealthier than most others, and part of the charm of a high-status good may be its price.

It seems plausible that cocaine demand should be more price elastic than that for marijuana but that its elasticity, even in the long run, should remain below unity. If this were in fact the case, then total cocaine-dealing revenues would also increase with increasing enforcement.

There is no reason to believe that the price elasticity of drug demand will be invariant to the price itself; rather, the reverse is true: the lower the price, the less significant will be a given percentage change, relative to either consumers' budgets or to the cost of alternative goods, and thus, one would expect, the lower price elasticity of demand. (This may not be true if lower prices create new, particularly price-sensitive applications, as may often be the case in the world of producers' goods, but this caveat has no obvious application to drug use.) A 50 percent increase in the cost of a five dollar joint ought to be far more noticeable, even to those still in the marijuana market in that price range, than a 50 percent increase in the price of today's fifty-cent joint.

For any drug, presumably there is some level of enforcement— not necessarily one achievable with plausible resources under existing institutional arrangements—where the price is driven high enough that price elasticity of demand goes past unity and total revenues begin to fall as price rises. At the extreme, sufficiently high levels of enforcement vigilance and sufficiently draconian punishments might suffice to drive the market out of existence altogether.

Trafficking Revenues and Trafficking Crime

If tighter drug enforcement makes the dollar volume of the market grow, business and enforcement crime should grow along with it. With more money at stake, there is more to fight about, more to extort, more to steal, more to guard. With greater enforcement risks, there is more occasion to use violence against potential witnesses. As the level of offensive and defensive violence within the industry increases, those participants least able or willing to use violence will find themselves at a disadvantage; the value of the command of violence, relative to other business assets and skills, will grow. (As the trade becomes more violence intensive, the producers to whom violence is available at low cost are advantaged in relation to those to whom it is more expensive.) This squeezing out of the relatively peaceful will make the trade even more dangerous and thus feed on itself. It therefore appears that successful drug enforcement, up to the point where the price elasticity of demand exceeds unity, will tend to increase the levels of trafficking-related ancillary crime by increasing both the dollar value of the traffic and the market shares of traffickers who rely most heavily on violence and corruption.

Trafficking-related crime will thus find its minimum at two opposite points on the enforcement continnuum: perfect enforcement, where there is no trafficking because there is no market for the commodity at the risk-covering price, and unrestricted legalization, where producers and purveyors of the substance are no more likely to be perpetrators or victims of crime than other merchants.

Almost any form of regulation, including taxation, will generate ancillary crime: tax evasion, violation of regulations (saloons serving minors or keeping open after hours), and bribery of regulatory and licensing officials. Imposition of a state monopoly, particularly at only one level of the trade, will lead to other sorts of bribery and corruption, as in the case of the bribery of purchasing agents for state monopoly liquor stores by distributors of particular brands of liquor.

There may be certain forms of regulation that create no opportunities for profitable violation or evasion. Bans or restrictions on advertising, for example, may tend to be virtually self-enforcing because advertising is by its nature difficult to conceal. The more vice regulation works through regulations that leave no niche for profitable violation, the smaller the problem it will create in the form of trafficking-related crime in general and organized crime in particular.

Drug Enforcement and Organized Crime

What are the effects of the level and tactics of the drug enforcement effort on the magnitude of the organized crime problem?

Organized Crime and the Vice Markets

Thomas C. Schelling has suggested that, under quite plausible conditions, the existence of organized crime might be of service to the suppression of vice by keeping prices higher than they would otherwise be (Schelling, 1971). The present line of argument suggests the converse, that government efforts to suppress vice are likely to be of service to organized crime. Schelling conceives of organized crime as an organization or group of organizations with the ability and willingness to use violence against participants in the vice trades and that use that ability to commit extortion and/or create a cartel structure for those trades. Since the result of these activities is a combination of increased costs for vice-providing firms and the creation of oligopoly rents, consumers pay higher prices. At higher prices, they demand a lower quantity of illicit goods and services than they would at the prices that would prevail in the absence of organized crime. Thus, from the limited perspective of cutting down on the consumption of gambling, prostitution, drugs, and the like, law enforcement and organized crime have effects tending in the same direction.

This chapter starts with a somewhat different conception of organized crime. While Mafia families (and other groups with different organizational histories and ethnic makeups but similarly elaborate internal structures and similarly long organizational time horizons) may well have the capacities for violence that Schelling attributes to them, although Peter Reuter suggests that at least some of them are likely to have instead no-longer-deserved reputations for such capacities (Reuter 1983a: 134), they are likely to differ from Schelling's corporate-style extortionist/cartel organizers in at least two ways. First, they are likely to resemble trade associations or political machines rather than corporations or partnerships in terms of how decisions are made and financial gains divided. Second, the earnings of the persons making up the organization are likely to be less from the purely parasitic activities of extortion and cartel organization than from the productive activities of buying, selling, organizing, and (again following Reuter) providing contract-enforcement and dispute-resolution services to vice-market participants.

This is not to suggest that straight extortion and cartel organization (under the rubric of "street tax") are unknown or important or that competitors of organized crime figures and suppliers, customers, and employees with whom organized crime figures have business disputes are not in danger of having violence inflicted on them. But it is to say that organized crime is more a participant in than a parasite on the markets it shares.

In Schelling's model, the key element that allows organized crime to feed off an industry is that industry's illegality, which makes it impossible for participants to call the police when the extortionists come around. Beyond that simple fact of illegality, the degree of enforcement would not seem to have much impact on the degree of organized crime influence in an illicit trade. If organized crime is able to organize a cratel and set the consumer price to yield the largest possible cartel rent, then cost increases introduced by enforcement pressure will necessarily reduce that rent. If, on the other hand, organized crime groups are participants in uncartelized markets, the effects on them of increased enforcement pressure are less clear.

Defining Organized Crime

Any discussion of the effects of varying levels of drug enforcement on organized crime needs to make an elementary definitional distinction that is sometimes ignored. A definition of the term *organized crime* can serve any of three quite distinct objectives. It can be descriptive: a hypothesis about the nature of the Mafia. It can be theoretical: the creation of an ideal type—like the firm of economic theory—about which precise reasoning is possible but whose relationship to actual phenomena remains to be explored. It can be evaluative: a sketch of the characteristics of certain actual or hypothetical criminal organizations that make them the worthy objects of a particular kind of social concern.

The test of a descriptive definition is whether it fits the facts. The test of a theoretical definition is whether it leads to interesting results and whether the ideal type bears enough resemblance to some part of reality to make the results meaningful. The test of an evaluative definition is whether it points up the right set of concerns. A great deal of the confusion that characterizes discussions of organized crime seems to stem from the difficulty in distinguishing propositions about the Mafia from propositions about all the entities that fit some theoretical or evaluative definition of organized crime.

This is not a purely academic matter. The federal government has recently launched a major effort directed at organized crime and drug trafficking. Much of the internal and external rhetoric about the program appealed to the need to fight the mob as justification for a drug-enforcement push. The implicit line of reasoning is (1) for various reasons, the wealth and power of the Mafia and its associates is a problem; (2) the size of the illicit drug markets means that they are or may become a significant source of that wealth and power; (3) therefore a major effort should be directed at Mafia-related drug-trafficking activities as part of the organized crime effort.

This represents a notable reversal from the classical line that the Mafia is to be fought at all costs because it is responsible for drug importation, but there is no direct contradiction involved. it might be the case that the revenues to be gained from marijuana and cocaine trafficking could help shore up the heroin-importing business. But current enforcement rhetoric treats all major drug trafficking as organized crime because it involves major organizations that are now sometimes referred to as organized drug-trafficking cartels.

The confusion between the ideal-type organized crime (as represented by National Organized Crime Planning Council or the General Accounting Office definition of that term) and the actual Mafia may lead to a set of counterproductive policies. Justified by the need to crack down on the mob, they are likely instead to result in making the drug markets more hospitable to, and more lucrative for, organized crime groups. This will apply both to the traditional families and to other organizations with different ethnic bases, which share many of the Mafia's most unpleasant characteristics and which might come to share even more of them under the new enforcement.

Organized Crime and the Drug Markets

The traffic in illicit drugs is the largest source of revenue for large criminal organizations. A significant fraction (perhaps 20 percent) of the $10 billion to $30 billion Americans spend every year on various contraband drugs is the value added at the top of the trade.[2] Some unknown additional fraction goes to lower-level distribution organizations that are more than simple agglomerations of persons in the habit of buying and selling to one another and that have some of the characteristics of enterprises.

These revenues do not go primarily to organized crime, if that phrase is used as simply an ethnically neutral synonym for "Mafia."

While two of New York's "five families" are reportedly a significant or even dominant factor in the importation of heroin from Italy into New York, no other Mafia group is reported to play a noticeable role in any other drug market. The intensity of the national organized crime enforcement effort and the stiff sentences handed out for mob-connected drug dealing may account for this. Except for the extraordinary circumstances of the European heroin connections, Mafia organizations may simply be high-cost producers in the drug-dealing industry. The proposition that the Mafia is not important in drug dealing does not imply the converse; drug dealing may be very important to some parts of the Mafia. Even a small part of a $20 billion retail market may be an attractive alternative to booking horse bets and chiseling on union dental plans.

But most of the discussion about drug dealing and organized crime concerns the growth of new criminals organizations with Mafia-like characteristics: long organizational life, a readiness to use violence in business dealings and against potential witnesses, resistance to penetration by undercover agents, influence over local politicians and law enforcement, and a willingness to engage in a wide variety of criminal activities in addition to drug dealing. The model is the growth of the Mafia during prohibition, when the availability of bootlegging money catalyzed major changes in the structure of the underworld, which outlasted the end of prohibition itself. The examples are the outlaw motorcycle gangs, which now have major shares in the market for synthetic stimulants and hallucinogens (dexamphetamine, methamphetamine, PCP, LSD) and the Herrera family, which is said to be vertically integrated in the heroin industry from Mexican poppy field to Chicago street corner.

From the proposition that the drug trade is creating the criminal empires of tomorrow, one might draw the inference that more vigorous drug enforcement can, in Churchill's phrase, "strangle the baby in its crib," or, less dramatically, that one benefit of devoting more resources to drug enforcement would be preventing or retarding the growth of emerging criminal enterprises. Indeed the documents and speeches surrounding the creation of the new organized crime–drug trafficking forces emphasized the threat of organized crime (clearly in more than its Mafia sense), as well as the threat of drug consumption itself as a reason to devote new resources to the drug-enforcement effort.

But if the effect of successful drug enforcement is to increase the total revenues of drug traffickers and to increase the value of the ability to use violence to transact business and to thwart investigations and prosecution, then this strategy will be self-defeating.

Both the overall value of the drug markets and the advantages enjoyed within them by the most dangerous groups will increase.

This thesis—that increased enforcement pressure directed at the top level of the drug markets will increase the wealth, power, and dangerousness of high-level drug-dealing organizations—may seem to be a paradox, the sort of deliberately perverse argument for which law enforcement intellectuals are notorious among law enforcement practitioners. How can one make a group of people better off by throwing more of them in prison? There are three levels of answer to this objection.

First, the focus here is not on the overall well-being—the utility position—of drug dealers but on their dollar revenues, their wealth, and their ability and incentive to use violence and corruption to transact business and avoid punishment. Logically it would be possible for increased enforcement to make organized criminals uniformly worse off and uniformly wealthier, more powerful, and more dangerous.

Second, some criminals get caught; others do not. To some extent, this is a random process or appears random until the outcomes re known. A lottery where some of the proceeds go as expenses and profits to the organizers makes lottery ticket buyers as a group poorer, but it makes the winners richer. Similarly increased enforcement could reduce the utility position of organized crime participants as a group, and thus the lifetime expected-value welfare of each individual who chooses to try his or her hand at high-level crime, yet increase not only the dollar wealth but the overall welfare of successful (on this hypothesis, merely lucky) organized criminals. If the hope of becoming a wealthy racketeer were an important influence on the choice of a criminal career—if the wealthy Mafia don served as a role model for the street mugger—the supply of such role models would be increased, not decreased, by such a lottery-like process.

Finally, if risk aversion, skill at evading punishment, and disutility for prison time are unequally distributed across the population of potential law breakers, those who are most highly skilled, least risk averse, and least bothered by the prospect of prison may be the net beneficiaries, even in an expected-utility sense, from increases in enforcement that improve their market position relative to more cautious, more sensitive, and less skilled competitors (Moore 1973; Spence 1977).

If none of this seems persuasive, consider the following argument from the extreme case: the extreme of law enforcement is legalization. What is the current role of the Mafia in the market for liquor? If the existence of vice laws creates opportunities for organized crime, there is no paradox in suggesting that their vigorous enforcement may expand those opportunities. If trafficking-related crime finds a minimum at unregulated legalization and if the world of crime obeys the mean value theorem, then there must be a region over which increasing enforcement yields an increase in crime.

Trafficking-Related Crime under Decreasing Enforcement

Decreases in enforcement pressure on an illicit market would lead to decreases in the trafficking revenues available, which might tend to increase the level of business violence (in the form of turf wars or of violence related to cartel formation and enforcement) as competitors struggle to maintain their revenues in a shrinking (in dollar terms) market. Neither possibility can be ruled out. Competitive violence has been known to result from industry shrinkage—perhaps the best-known example is the trucking industry violence of the early years of the Great Depression—and the relatively low level of enforcement activity under prohibition did not prevent the sanguinary beer wars. Industries sufficiently illegal so that participants cannot call the police but under slight enough enforcement pressure to allow relatively open operations without heavy physical security (these might be called slightly illegal industries) might seem ideal targets for robbery, extortion, or attempts at cartel formation.

But none of the illicit drug industries seems well suited to the growth of business violence in the absence of enforcement pressure. Under what conditions will shrinking revenues increase the incentives for competitive violence? The revelant condition would seem to be that the marginal value of a revenue dollar grows faster than the market shrinks, so that the importance of the game increases as the monetary stakes get lower. This condition will be characteristic of industries with high fixed costs, such as the trucking industry where the capital costs of the trucks need to be met or the garment industry where a skilled work force needs to be kept busy. In such industries an unexpected shrinkage in the overall market can convert competition for market share into a fight for survival, and both have been characterized by violent attempts to gain competitive advantage or enforce minimum prices. Similar fixed-cost pressures formed the backdrop for the switchgear price-fixing cases.

The drug markets do not seem to be characterized by such a high level of fixed costs. "Firms" rapidly form, grow, shrink, disappear, and reemerge, and even the roles of entrepreneur, agent, service provider, and employee, as well as those of buyer, seller, and broker, seem to be fluid. While little is known about the organization of mid-level and low-level drug dealing, particularly for marijuana and cocaine, vigorous competition among many providers seems to be the rule. Neither the threat of fixed costs and idle assets leading to insolvency nor the opportunity provided by a well-defined industry structure seems to be present.

Moreover, the very high value-to-weight and value-to-bulk ratios of illicit drugs, though they encourage thefts of the drugs themselves, tend to discourage the competitive violence of the beer wars variety by eliminating tactically attractive targets. A cocaine distributor has no distillery, no large fixed warehouse, no trucks, no physical retail establishments on the model of speakeasies; perhaps not even any employees, certainly not an army of brawny truckdrivers and deliverymen. Even marijuana, by far the bulkiest of the illicit drugs, is far more compact than alcohol; a $5 pint of whiskey and a $500 pound of marijuana weight the same, net packaging, and the marijuana takes up far less room than a six-pack of beer.

Thus the relatively low-grade business violence of slashed tires, shattered windows, and burned trucks has no analogue in the illicit drug trade, and systematic hijacking is infinitely more difficult because the goods are so much easier to conceal. If business disputes are to take a violent turn, there is no easy ladder of escalation to climb, no small change in the currency of unfriendly acts, and perhaps not even convenient proxies to inflict and absorb personal violence while the principals negotiate. This should tend to reduce the frequency with which disputes turn violent by inadvertence and limit business violence to those disputes where the principals are willing to run the risks of trying to kill each other, with the dispute resembling a duel more than a war. Other things being equal, this should reduce the total number of violent disputes.

Effects on Criminal Labor Markets

This analysis does not take into account the effects of drug trafficking on the market for criminal labor and entrepreneurship and thus on the supply of members and associates for organized crime groups. That relationship is a tangled one, and not much of evaluative significance can be said a priori.

A simple static model would have criminals choosing their next crime (or career segment) from the selection generated by the laws and by enforcement strategies, balancing income and risk; bank robbery is one choice, selling cocaine another. A drug enforcement strategy that reduced the opportunities in the drug trade would then make additional labor available for other criminal enterprises. Even if—as seems likely—the number of criminals varies with the opportunities available, so that the drug trade draws its labor supply partly from other criminal endeavors and partly from the licit economy, it would still be the case (if the willingness to commit crimes is unevenly distributed) that drug crimes compete with other crimes in the labor market. If this were true, a flourishing illicit drug industry would reduce the level of other crimes requiring similar inputs of labor.

But if breaking the law is an individual and organizational habit or if having once been a criminal for a living reduces one's licit opportunities and/or increases one's criminal opportunities, then a flourishing drug trade, by attracting honest people into the criminal labor force, will increase the overall criminal labor force for the future. A subsequent decrease in drug-related criminal opportunities would then create an underemployed criminal class and thus increases in nondrug crime. Whether existing organized crime groups would benefit from the decrease in the price of criminal labor or suffer from an increase in competition depends in part on their internal structure and the nature of the enterprises in which they engage and in part on the ratio of chiefs to Indians in the additional supply of criminals. However, whatever an increase in the criminal labor supply might do to the welfare of current organized crime members and associates, it would certainly worsen the extent of the organized crime problem from a social viewpoint.

Implications for Enforcement Policy

This argument leads to two distinct policy conclusions. First, effects on the growth of dangerous criminal organizations are put on the cost side rather than the benefit side of the drug enforcement ledger. The question about increasing attention to drug enforcement becomes, Do the benefits of decreased drug consumption outweigh the costs of increased wealth and power for major dealing organizations? For drugs like marijuana and cocaine, the answer may be equivocal.

Second, the analysis suggests a need to design drug enforcement efforts in ways that minimize the growth of ongoing violent groups. This may involve some counterintuitive steps. For example, a focus on high-level dealing will increase the returns to successful high-level dealing and the value of tight organization, while a focus on lower-level dealers and users will reduce wholesale prices—which are the revenues of high-level dealers—and perhaps reduce the quantity sold.

If a simple strategy of aggressive enforcement against high-level drug dealers is likely to increase the wealth and power of organized crime, it makes sense to inquire whether there exist alternative drug enforcement strategies that lack this unfortunate side effect or that positively contribute to the organized crime control effort.

Targeting High-Level Enforcement

One obvious answer is to target drug enforcement efforts at persons thought to be involved with already recognized organized crime groups and at drug-dealing organizations with the organized crime characteristics of significant internal structure, continuity over time, and the ability and willingness to use violence, intimidation, and corruption to resist enforcement efforts. This prescription is largely consonant with the intentions of past practice and current policy at the federal level. Drug cases against mafiosi have long been treated as part of the organized crime enforcement effort and evaluated with respect to the importance of the persons to be charged rather than the significance to the drug markets of the quantities of drugs involved. The current organized crime/drug enforcement task force program intends to take a similar approach with respect to groups primarily engaged in drug trafficking that threaten to develop Mafia-like characteristics.

This approach raises two questions. First, is it consistent with a serious attempt to reduce the size of the markets for illicit drugs, or will it mean that great resources are expended to convict the leaders of the most threatening groups while the overall traffic flourishes? If the latter, the alternative of deemphasizing marijuana and cocaine enforcement may do better at checking the growth of organized crime groups (simply by shrinking their opportunities) with about the same effect on drug consumption. Second, does an adequate intelligence base exist with respect to what are sometimes called emerging organized crime groups to allow, as a practical matter, a focus on organizations rather than drug flows? Does anyone know enough about the various individuals and groups at the top of the cocaine trade to distinguish bad from merely big? Will there be any operational difference between going after major cocaine dealers and going after emerging organized crime groups based on the cocaine trade? If not, and if the previous analysis has been correct, then the problem remains.

Targeting Activities Rather Than Groups

A slightly more subtle approach, applicable even if the identities of the most dangerous groups and their participants are unknown, would be to target the activities that make organized crime a different problem from conspiracy: violence and the obstruction of justice. This could be done directly—by stressing murder, witness intimidation, enforcement corruption, and perjury charges rather than drug or drug conspiracy counts, in indictments—or indirectly—by using intelligence about such activities to select priority targets for investigation and prosecution on whatever charges prove best. That is, if we are worried that intensive drug enforcement will create competitive advantages for those groups best able to obstruct the enforcement process, we should set out to create competitive disadvantages for such groups. Insofar as we know who they are in advance, this can be done by targeting them directly; insofar as they start out unknown to us, then it must be done by allowing them to target themselves by engaging in the activities we fear. In either case, the result will be a drug-enforcement program whose most important targets may not be the most important drug dealers. Operating such a program with agents and agencies used to measuring the importance of a drug enforcement target by drug type and quantity may pose very difficult management problems.

Alternatively we could attempt to alter the structure of the drug markets so as to make them less profitable at the top. High-level enforcement pressure at the top would seem to have the opposite effect. Enforcement pressure lower down, however, ought to make top-level dealing less profitable by raising retail prices (as lower-level dealers require higher margins to compensate for increased risk) and thus reducing the quantity purchased at any given wholesale price level.

Dynamics of Retail Drug Dealing

In certain species there is a critical level of population below which the species is not self-sustaining; since mating relies on chance encounters between males and females, below some critical population, the number of meetings per female falls below replacement level. Retail drug dealing may behave analogously. The probability that cruising around will lead to a successful meeting depends on the number of buyers and sellers in the market in a given region. But the number of buyers and sellers itself depends in part on the probability of a successful meeting: the search time to score from the buyer's perspective, the waiting time between customers from the seller's.

Like other market situations, this one may tend to equilibrate and bounce back from small perturbations. A small decrease in the number of heroin sellers at Ninth and O streets, N.W., in Washington, D.C., would create opportunities for new sellers to enter the market since there would be, at least at first, a surplus of unsatisfied buyers. By the same token, a decrease in the number of buyers might lead some sellers to be a little more open and a little less cautious about dealing with strangers, thus decreasing search times for novice users and effectively increasing the number of buyers.

But a system that resists small and temporary perturbations may be less resilient in the face of larger and longer-lasting ones. Imagine that all of the heroin sellers at that street corner vanished and were not replaced for two months. Once it became known within the heroin-consuming population that Ninth and O was no longer a place to score, people would start to look for another street corner. At the end of two months, a dealer who tried to resume business at Ninth and O would probably find that his customers were elsewhere. That being so, the dealer would move to where the density of buyers was greater. A temporary change in conditions might produce a shift in the location of the market capable of outlasting the original change.

Within a city, both buyers and sellers are mobile. This is less true between cities, but the problem of needing buyers to attract sellers and sellers to attract buyers is the same. As a result, the place to be a heroin buyer is where there are already many sellers, and the place to be a heroin seller is where there are already many buyers. The only heroin dealer in Muskogee would have a monopoly, to be sure, but not a profitable one, because he would have no customers. That being so, the absence of any such dealer does not create a market niche waiting to be filled. By the same token, if there is someone in Muskogee waiting on the corner to score some heroin, he will wait a long time. This condition suggests that the user population in Muskogee is unlikely to grow since being a user is not a practical proposition.

Many buyers/many sellers and no buyers/no sellers are thus both stable equilibria. The tendencies of the enforcement system may act to reinforce the tendency of going markets to continue and new markets not to appear. If there were a heroin seller in Muskogee, he would be the most important drug enforcement target in the county, and the district attorney and the U.S. attorney probably would fight about who got to prosecute the case. Convincing the judge to hand out a stiff sentence would not be difficult. By contrast, in the District of Columbia, the U.S. attorney's office (which also prosecutes state charges in D.C. superior court) will not even prosecute a heroin trafficking case without two undercover buys from the same dealer.

The combination of market and enforcement forces may help explain why the heroin problem is almost entirely a big city problem.

In the tendency of the enforcement system to pay more attention to a drug dealer of a given size where drug dealing is scarce than to the same size dealer where drug dealing is common, we have at last discovered a feature of the system that is not perverse. The first heroin dealer in town is much less likely to be replaced than the two hundredth, or even the tenth, because a one-dealer town may well not have developed a user group large enough to pay the start-up costs of a potential replacement.

Value of Street-Level Enforcement

Keeping drug dealing out where it does not now exist is therefore an enforcement goal likely to be attainable within available resources. Ending—rather than merely moving—drug marketplaces in cities where they are well entrenched is likely to be a much more expensive project with much dimmer prospects. But there is value in keeping retail drug markets small and discreet even if they cannot be eliminated.

The basic problem of vice enforcement is that the price that discourages the buyer is also the revenue that encourages the trafficker. But this is true only of the money price. The other components of what Mark Moore has called the effective price—search time and risk—are dead-weight loss, expended by the purchaser but not accruing to the seller (Moore 1973). Moreover, since the cost is not in dollars, it does not increase the buyer's needs for income. The buyer may thus shift his or her efforts from making money to searching for a connection and wind up spending less money and consuming less heroin. If this happens to consumers in general, drug wholesalers will find their incomes shrinking as volumes and pricess fall; from their perspective, an increase in consumer search time will look like an unexplained drop in demand.

Enforcement against drug importers and distributors affects the price of drugs without much affecting the number and behavior of retailers. Retail—street-level—drug enforcement, by making dealers keep their heads down and causing them to be wary about whom they deal with, increases search time. Mark Moore has noted that under conditions of vigorous street-level enforcement, new drug users have particular difficulty in scoring, and this too is all to the good (Moore 1973). Thus, while top-level drug enforcement makes drug users more dangerous and organized criminals richer, effective street-level enforcement reduces drug use and the need for money by drug users while at the same time hurting high-level drug dealers in their bank accounts.

Resources and Perceived Justice

Although street enforcement strategies aimed at marijuana and co-caine would be more expensive than a similar strategy aimed at heroin, no street-level strategy would be cheap. There would have to be available large numbers of jail and prison cells or substantial other punishment capacity if an increased number of retail-dealing arrests were to have any effect on dealers other than the inconven-ience of arrest and the confiscation of their immediate stock.

With the total national confinement capacity at about 600,000 and with confinement capacity the binding constraint on the law enforcement system, a street-level enforcement program that did not include a new supply of punishment capacity would either collapse for lack of anything to do with convicted dealers or result in reduced sanctions for other forms of lawbreaking. The former seems the more likely outcome if judges and parole boards are given the choice be-tween freeing low-level drug dealers and freeing more obviously pred-atory criminals.

Part of the problem is that although street-level dealers as a class may be very important, an individual street-level dealer does not look like a very bad person. Although criminal law enforcement can be used for regulatory purposes, it is, as a process and in the eyes of its participants, not regulatory but retributive. Criminal justice looks backward to past individual wrongdoing and not forward to future social outcomes. This distinction between the ultimate goals of a policy and the immediate objectives of its execution is common to all processes that rely on making and carrying out threats, but the criminal justice system introduces notions of individual responsi-bility and deserved punishment that are more demanding than the notion of carrying out a threat. Going after small wrongdoers while largely ignoring big ones may be sensible regulation, but it is not visible justice.

Thus, a policy of aggressive street level enforcement will need a good supply of nonprison sanctions, both to economize on prison and jail space and to convince judges that the punishments they are asked to impose are proportionate to the crimes committed. Home confinement and community service programs are possibilities, and they could be combined, with a convict being required to stay at home except when working. Community service need not mean making speeches to civic groups or working in the office of the judge's favorite charity; communities can also be served with picks and shovels.

Demand Reduction

The wealth of drug traffickers and the frustration of drug enforcers rest on the fact that millions of consumers want illicit drugs. Anything that tends to depress demand will reduce both trafficking-related ancillary crime and the level of drug enforcement resources needed to attain any given level of reduction in drug consumption. The idea of a strategy against drug trafficking and organized crime suggests wiretaps and prison cells, but the real war might best be waged with propaganda directed at users.[3]

The recent Rand Corporation report, "Strategies for Controlling Adolescent Drug Use," argues that junior high school antidrug programs based on a social-pressures model of drug use could significantly reduce the fraction of adolescents who become regular marijuana users and that doing so would probably have significant spillover effects on the use of other illicit drugs (Polich et al. 1984:152). The Rand report goes on to argue that such efforts are likely to be more cost-effective in reducing drug consumption, at least among adolescents, than enforcement programs. Whether this latter proposition is correct, demand reduction is clearly the strategy of choice with respect to its effects on organized crime.

Notes

1. 5,000 metric tons = 5 million kilograms = 5 billion grams. At 0.4 grams per joint, 5 billion grams = 12.5 billion joints. 12.5 billion joints/year for 20 million users = 625 joints/user/year or 1.7 + joints/user/day.

2. Only about 10 percent of the price of heroin and cocaine is accounted for by their prices at first domestic sale. The fraction for marijuana is much higher, about 40 percent.

3. Spraying paraquat on growing marijuana should probably also be considered as a demand reduction strategy since its effect on users' fears is likely to be far more significant than its (almost certainly slight) impact on supply. Of course, this aspect of the paraquat issue raises serious questions, both about whether the proper balance between the risk of users' health and the benefits achieved in reducing marijuana consumption and trafficking and about the ethics of government actions which may damage illicit-

market consumers. Controls on the sale of hypodermic syringes have the same relation to the heroin market as paraquat spraying does to the marijuana market: reducing consumption while threatening the health of the remaining users.

References

Moore, Mark H. 1977. *Buy and Bust: The Effective Regulation of an Illicit Market in Heroin*. Lexington, Mass.: Lexington Books.

––––––. 1973. "Policies to Achieve Discrimination on the Effective Price of Heroin." *American Economic Review* 63, no. 2 (May).

Polich, J. Michael; Phyllis L. Ellickson; Peter Reuter; and James P. Kahan. 1984. *Strategies for Controlling Adolescent Drug Use*. Santa Monica, Calif.: Rand Corporation.

Reuter, Peter. 1983a. *Disorganized Crime*. Cambridge: MIT Press.

––––––. 1983b. "Risks and Prices: The Economics of Drug Enforcement." Paper presented to the Annual Conference of the Association for Public Policy Analysis and Management, Philadelphia, October 14.

Schelling, Thomas C. 1977. "What is the Business of Organized Crime?" *Journal of Public Law* 20.

Spence, A. Michael. 1977. "A Note on the Effects of Pressure in the Heroin Market." Discussion Paper 588. Cambridge: Harvard Institute of Economic Research, November.

6
Organized Crime and Politics

Herbert E. Alexander

I n my specialty of money in elections, I have had two official
occasions, and numerous others, to try to relate organized crime
and political contributions, a hidden relationship about which
there is too little sunshine, public reporting, disclosure, or knowledge. In 1968 I authored a background paper for the National Commission on the Causes and Prevention of Violent. In 1973 I wrote a
background paper for the National Advisory Commission on Criminal Justice Standards and Goals.[1]

On each of those occasions, as well as in other instances when
I have considered this relationship, I found it necessary to write in
general about the uses and abuses of political money but to focus
specifically on the opportunities provided by the U.S. political system—at federal, state, and local levels—for organized crime to relate
in legal or illegal ways with candidates for public office and with
office-holders and leaders of political parties.[2] In that sense my earlier
efforts, along with this present one, represent a commentary on omissions in political studies and investigations. There are numerous
studies of corrupt politicians but not of their connections with organized crime.

Illustrations abound of the uses and abuses of political contributions in ways that make for an unhealthy political environment.
The seamy side of campaign financing achieves occasional headlines
but sufficient prominence to create the impression that political
money is more often tainted than not. This contributes to public
cynicism about political money and also affects basic citizen attitudes toward politicians and the entire political process. To the degree that unhealthy attitudes persist, political parties and candidates
may have difficulty in raising sufficient funds from legitimate sources
and hence may be tempted to turn to funds from questionable sources.

Several examples of organized criminal involvement in election
campaign financing or in buying favors from office-holders have come
to light.[3] Richard Hatcher, the first black mayor of Gary, Indiana,

reported that criminal elements offered him $100,000 not to contest the Democratic primary against the entrenched machine that afforded them protection. After refusing and winning the primary, he was offered an identical amount for an agreement to permit gambling and other rackets if elected, which he again refused. In New Jersey, monitored mobsters' conversations revealed that underworld money flowed copiously into the campaign of Hugh J. Addonizio, a former congressman who was elected mayor of Newark and was later convicted on charges of sharing kickbacks extorted from contractors doing business with the city. Bribes and kickbacks paid by contractors to city officials in Reading, Pennsylvania, given in the guise of campaign contributions, found their way in numerous cases into the officials' pockets rather than party or campaign coffers, where the transactions nevertheless would have been illegal.

More recently, investigations of the toxic-waste industry have led law enforcement officers to conclude that it is becoming increasingly dominated by organized crime.[4] The result has been the secret and illegal dumping of large quantities of dangerous chemicals. Some of this illicit disposal allegedly has been accomplished with the cooperation of public officials. One waste contractor, Charles Macaluso, stood trial in 1983 on charges of bribing local New Jersey officials in connection with a municipal disposal contract for one of his companies.[5] Macaluso had been one of three honorary co-hosts for the 1976 Democratic National Convention in New York. Late in 1982 Allen M. Dorfman, a wealthy insurance executive, and Roy I. Williams, president of the International Brotherhood of Teamsters, were convicted on charges of attempting to bribe Howard W. Cannon, then a Democratic senator from Nevada. Cannon was not indicted but subsequently lost his Senate seat. Dorfman and Williams were alleged to have underworld ties.[6]

In addition to examples of corruption of political candidates and public officials by organized crime, often through bribes disguised as campaign contributions, there are numerous instances of extortion and conspiracy on the part of greedy or needy politicians seeking to exchange campaign money for favors or preferment. A former New Jersey secretary of state, a Democrat, was convicted on federal charges of bribery and extortion for seeking $10,000 in political contributions at a time when he was organizing a gubernatorial campaign from a company that sought a contract to build a bridge. His successor, a Republican, also was convicted of extorting $10,000 in political contributions for the state Republican party in return for attempting to fix the awarding of a state highway construction contract. Also convicted were a prominent party fund raiser and the president of the construction company that allegedly made the contribution.[7] Clearly corruption crosses party lines, but it is not necessarily corruption related to organized crime.

Still another example of the malignant links that can develop between money and politics is the case of former Vice-President Spiro Agnew. Routine investigations of corruption in Baltimore County, where Agnew had been county executive, uncovered a pattern of contributions to Agnew from persons already under investigation for alleged kickbacks and bribes. Evidence led to the grand jury indictment of Agnew for alleged bribery, extortion, and tax fraud. Witnesses alleged that Agnew had pocketed well over $100,000, claiming the money to be campaign contributions, by using his political office to hand out county and state contracts in exchange for personal payoffs from seven engineering firms and one financial institution. Agnew's resignation from office was one of the conditions of a plea-bargaining agreement under which he pleaded no contest to a single count of tax evasion.[8] Although not an example of corruption related to organized crime, the Agnew case illustrates the fine line between outright bribery and campaign contributions. The line may often be thin, but where there is detailed accounting of campaign funds or of sources of income, it is more difficult to rationalize that the one was meant to be the other. Statutory disclosure brings at least some discipline to transactions involving money and elected public officials, and if laws are enforced, even greater discipline results.

Nevertheless, it is often the case that those who are detected in violations are punished, if at all, for tax fraud, extortion, conspiracy, larceny, or bribery but rarely for stretching an already flexible code of campaign finance. It may be assumed that until some candidate, campaign managers, treasurers, and contributors are severly punished for the evident white-collar violations of election laws, the old habits of laxity will persist.

The extent to which contributions are bound up with expressed or tacit obligations cannot be measured, but it is undoubtedly greater at the state and local levels than at the federal level. Not only criminal elements but respectable business persons and professionals use campaign contributions to obtain favors and preferment regarding contracts, jobs, taxation, zoning, and numerous other action-laden areas of government. Some relationships are openly acknowledged. In many places systematic solicitation of those who benefit from the system occurs. In some cases, contributions are made to both parties as a hedge, seeking to purchase goodwill and access, if not actual contracts, regardless of who is elected.

But even where there is no clear-cut official malfeasance, it may be customary for the beneficiary of government favor to show gratitude by contributing. For example, in Illinois, $100,000 in contributions to Illinois Republicans was revealed to have come from corporations interconnected with two racetrack companies granted licenses by the Illinois Racing Board. The board was controlled by Republicans. The contributions were made some twenty days after the board granted the licenses, which had followed an extensive inquiry into fitness to hold a license. The contributing firms were controlled by a man who was known as a generous contributor to Democratic politics in New Jersey, where he lived. It was later revealed that some $5,500 also had been contributed to Illinois Democrats. Although one of the contributing corporations later was fined for violating a prohibition of contributions from liquor licensees—the racetrack companies also held such licenses—no other prosecutions ensued. The case of former Illinois Governor Otto Kerner also involved racing.[9] Again, both parties were culpable.

An official choosing between two persons for an appointment or a contract is naturally more inclined toward the contributor than toward the stranger, toward the applicant or bidder who promises to supply campaign funds than the one who does not. Much of politics is built on a system of rewards, but the American system, which depends mainly on private financing, necessarily leads to favoritism. Even where civil service or bidding or other such laws make favoritism illegal, specifications can be rigged or inside information made available to the chosen.

In a pluralistic, democratic society like that of the United States, it is natural that individuals and groups with abundant economic resources will try to use their wealth to influence the course of government. Nevertheless, although money is a common denominator in shaping political power, other ingredients are vital as well: leadership, skill, information, public office, numbers of voters, public opinion.

Money is but one element in the equation of power. In the broadest sense, government is legitimized, and its future course largely determined, at the ballot box. People, not dollars, vote. But dollars help shape both voter behavior and governmental decisions. Individuals or groups with wealth use it to achieve policy goals by attempting to influence nominations or elections by promoting candidates with congenial views or by attempting to influence public officials. When wealthy persons seek to translate their economic power into political power, one of their tools may be money contributions.

Money is convertible into other resources; it may buy both goods and human energy and skills. But the converse also is true: other resources can be converted into political money, through use of rights pertaining to public office, for example, in awarding contracts and jobs, in controlling the flow of information, in making decisions. Skillful use of ideology, issues, and the perquisites and promises of office attract financial support to political actors in legitimate forms, as contributions and dues, or in illegitimate ways, as scandals from time to time have illustrated.

The amounts of money supplied by criminal elements, organized or otherwise, are a subject of universal curiosity, but there are few facts. Nevertheless, if organized crime has penetrated American society, as is often alleged, then the question follows whether organized criminal elements could operate as extensively without political sanctions at various levels of government. The question is troublesome, for in a complex governmental system with overlapping federal, state, and local jurisdictions and corresponding jealousies, many problems may fall between the cracks, leaving openings in which organized crime can operate with impunity. Clearly too little is known of political-criminal relationships, the incidences, the levels, the geographic areas, the impacts they have. Too little is known as well of the degree of cooperation among the many governmental units monitoring organized crime.

Part of the problem is the difficulty in distinguishing campaign gifts from other exchanges of money. The underworld has ample cash available with which members can and do seek protection, enter legitimate organizations or committees having political interests, insidiously muscle in or seek to influence the political or campaign decision-making processes, even monopolize the political processes in some areas.

Three decades ago the Second Interim Report of the Special Senate Committee to Investigate Organized Crime in Interstate Commerce (popularly called the Kefauver committee) concluded that one form of "corruption and connivance with organized crime in state and local government" is "contributions to the campaign funds of candidates for political office at various levels by organized criminals." Such criminal influence is bipartisan: "Not infrequently, contributions are made to both major political parties, gangsters operate on both sides of the street.[10] Little has occurred to revise this description. Widespread efforts undoubtedly continue on the part of criminal elements to seek political goodwill, access, and protection through generous political contributions.

The extent of such activity is unknown. More than two decades ago, scholars estimated that perhaps 15 percent of the money for state and local campaigns was derived from the underworld.[11] No better estimate exists today. Excluding the federal level, where the incidence of such behavior is presumed to be low, this would mean that almost $70 million might have come from criminal elements in 1980.[12]

The earlier estimate embraced funds given in small towns and rural areas by individuals operating on the borders of the law who wanted a sympathetic sheriff and prosecutor but who were not linked to crime syndicates. The estimate applied chiefly to persons engaged in illegal gambling and racketeering. It did not extend, for example, to otherwise reputable businesspersons who hoped for sympathetic treatment from building inspectors and tax assessors. At the time the estimate was made, organized crime also dealt with narcotics, which later became, however, a growth industry for amateur as well as professional criminal elements.

Two decades ago, at all levels of government, many electoral statutes invited criminal offenses but did little to discourage them. For too many years, in too many jurisdictions, too many candidates, election workers, and enforcement authorities tended to wink at certain election laws and make loose and strained legal interpretations designed to assist friends and opponents alike, to keep the rules of the game agreeable to fellow politicians. Unrealistic laws, particularly those regulating campaign finance, invited noncompliance. Laws that failed to take into account the clear need for political funds or the high stakes in winning elections led readily to noncompliance. In this atmosphere, criminal elements could exploit the political system.

Observers long knew that the American system of private financing of politics had its share of secret money, unreported money, criminal money, extorted money, laundered money, foreign money, tax-free money. They knew that there were many ways to spend money in support of candidates: through party, labor, business, professional, or miscellaneous committees, if not through candidate committees; through direct disbursements by the candidates or their families; by other individuals, not channeled through organized committees, as in independent expenditures; through issue organizations, from peace groups to gun lobbies. Since money will likely carve new channels when customary routes are restricted, reforms can readily become unenforceable and thus a mockery.

Although political financing in the United States was long undemocratic, with a strong tendency toward corruption, the system survived because for many years it managed to provide sufficient funds. Also, it served the purposes of certain special or corrupt interests. Nevertheless, the system increasingly came under attack, not only because of the collective weight of past corruptions but also because it no longer provided funds adequate to the needs of many campaigns. The increased incidence of deficit financing of campaigns in the 1960s was striking evidence of this failure.

Perhaps corrupt practices and government lawlessness have helped to create perceptions among many elements of the population that all politicians are shady and deceptive. The Watergate and Agnew cases may have reinforced that view. Consequently many individuals and groups became concerned about diminished confidence in the electoral process and accordingly examined every aspect of the process in an effort to devise ways of increasing levels of confidence, participation, relevance, and efficacy. During the 1970s and early 1980s, the election reform movement achieved significant changes in state and local election laws, requiring in all fifty of them much more detailed and comprehensive disclosure of political funds. No studies since have been conducted or recorded campaign gifts from criminal elements, perhaps because it is not likely even in the new climate that such money, if taken, would be disclosed or, if reported, be easily discernible. Many state laws now include, in addition to public reporting, prohibitions of cash contributions in excess of $50 or $100, and some thirty states have bipartisan commissions with responsibility to administer and enforce relevant election laws. The enforcement authority is civil, not criminal, but such commissions are charged to refer criminal matters to attorneys general, district attorneys, city prosecutors, and other appropriate enforcement officers. Whether these laws have made any difference in the matter of campaign gifts from organized criminal elements remains unknown. Of course, the risks involved now are greater for anyone, including the beneficiary candidate or party who would willfully violate the law, because exposure is more likely.

One index of the extent of political corruption exists in the compilation of *Federal Prosecutions of Corrupt Public Officials, 1970–1978*, a report issued by the U.S. Department of Justice.[13] More recent indexes may be found in annual reports on the activities of the Public Integrity Section of the Department of Justice, which are required by the Ethics in Government Act of 1978.[14] Although most of the prosecutions reported do not relate to political contributions but rather to fraud, bribery, and narcotics, the number of federal, state, and local public officials indicted under federal law in 1982 alone totaled 729.[15] If one were to add to that number prosecutions under state and local law, the figures would be far greater, indicating at least the susceptibility of some public officials to engage in prosecutable offenses.

Some light may be shed on the extent of organized criminal

involvement in electoral politics and public policymaking through investigations conducted by the Commission on Organized Crime established by President Ronald Reagan in mid-1983. Although the commission's mandate is far broader than determining the relationship between organized crime and campaign financing, commission chairman Judge Irving R. Kaufman of the U.S. Court of Appeals for the Second Circuit has said the commission would seek "a detailed understanding of how mobsters operate."[16] The commission's report is due to be submitted in March 1986. When the formation of the commission was announced, questions were raised by members of the press about the propriety of President Reagan's acceptance of support from the International Longshoremen's Union and the Teamsters, both of which have been linked to organized crime.[17]

Despite the strictures of the reform laws, if political money remains relatively scarce and alternative sources of financing are not readily available, the laws' prohibitions and limitations may get skirted. Too few laws at the federal or state level have been designed to assist candidates and parties in obtaining alternative sources of funds so that they need not rely on large contributions from special or corrupt interests.

Nineteen states have enacted forms of limited public financing (although two of them discontinued their programs), providing needed alternative funds when limits and prohibitions on contributions are imposed. Thirteen states have provided for the public monies through use of income tax checkoff systems similar to that of the federal government, and six have used tax surcharge procedures. The latter allow taxpayers to add a dollar or more to their tax liabilities, whereas the former allow taxpayers to earmark for a special political fund a dollar or two they would have to pay anyway. Hawaii, however, is the only state with a subsidy program that extends to candidates at the local level, where political contact with organized criminal elements is most likely to occur; but Hawaii provides such minimal amounts—as low as $50 per candidate—that candidates have not found sufficient relief from financial pressures to permit them to refuse contributions from unsavory sources. Most states that distribute money from public funds directly to candidates provide the money only for candidates for statewide offices. Only three of them also fund candidates for the state legislature, but the amounts provided are minimal. In a number of states in which public funds are distributed to political parties, the parties are permitted to use the money to support candidates for various offices, including the state legislature. But in those cases, too, the amounts available are small. The states have not been willing to commit the dollars that would be necessary to reduce financial pressures—and hence temptations—

on many state and local candidates for public office. Nor is there hope that the picture soon will change dramatically.

Political finance is an area of self-regulation by those affected, by those who have arrived successfully under the rules of the game. Incumbent legislators vote on proposals to improve the law and sometimes find ways to block signficant legislation before it gets to a vote. Potential prosecutors, attorneys general, and district attorneys are either elected or selected. They often are party loyalists who may be reluctant, under pressure of loyalty or gratitude, to enforce laws that traditionally have been underenforced.

Government lawlessness exists when ineffective laws are ineffectively enforced. By their tendency to inaction, governments establish an unfortunate climate: first because legislatures are reluctant to provide alternative sources of funds; second, because some incumbents who are self-righteous about their integrity but willingly excuse laxity with regard to their campaign finances are among the worst evaders and violators; and third, because some enforcement agents fail to do the job, which admittedly is difficult.[18] These factors lead readily to public cynicism. The impact on society cannot be calculated but must be presumed to be an important link in the chain of hypocrisy that is perceived by society in general and the less favored in particular. Levels of confidence in government are thereby lowered, creating alienation from the entire political process. This climate invites criminal participation in politics, and the occasional scandals testify to the nature and incidence of the continuing problem.

Notes

1. Herbert E. Alexander, "The Role of Money in the Political Process" (paper presented to the National Commission on the Causes and Prevention of Violence, Task Force on Law and Law Enforcement, October 1968), and "Goals and Standards for the Regulation of Political Finance" (paper prepared for the National Advisory Commission on Criminal Justice Standards and Goals, 1973).

2. See, for example, Herbert E. Alexander, "Watergate and the Electoral Process" (paper prepared for a conference of the U.S. Senate Select Committee on Presidential Campaign Activities and the Center for the Study of Democratic Institutions, Santa Barbara, California, December 9–12, 1973).

3. The following three examples are from Michael Dorman, *Payoff: The Role of Organized Crime in American Politics* (New York: David McKay Company, 1972), pp. 8–24, 47–48.

4. Ralph Blumenthal, "Illegal Dumping of Toxins Laid to Organized Crime," *New York Times*, June 5, 1983.

5. Ibid.

6. Ben A. Franklin, "Senate Panel Hears of Mob Link to Chicago Killing," *New York Times*, March 5, 1983.

7. For a discussion of these New Jersey and other state cases, see George Amick, *The American Way of Graft* (Princeton: Center for Analysis of Public Issues, 1979), pp. 125–130.

8. See *United States v. Spiro T. Agnew*, Crim. A. No. 73-0535, U.S. District Court, District of Maryland, October 10, 1973.

9. Amick, *American Way*, p. 235.

10. U.S. Congress, Senate, "Second Interim Report of the Special Senate Committee to Investigate Organized Crime in Interstate Commerce," 82d Cong., 1st sess., report no. 141, 1951, p. 1.

11. Alexander Heard, *The Costs of Democracy* (Chapel Hill: University of North Carolina Press, 1960), pp. 154–168; see also Donald R. Cressey, *Theft of the Nation: The Structure and Operations of Organized Crime in America* (New York: Harper & Row, 1969), p. 253.

12. Herbert E. Alexander, *Financing the 1980 Election* (Lexington, Mass.: Lexington Books, 1983), pp. 103–105.

13. *Federal Prosecutions of Corrupt Public Officials, 1970–1978*, report compiled by the Public Integrity Section, Criminal Division, U.S. Department of Justice (May 1, 1979), table X.

14. 28 U.S.C. 591 et seq.

15. "Report to Congress on the Activities and Operations of the Public Integrity Section for 1982," U.S. Department of Justice, (April 1983), p. 22.

16. Quoted in Leslie Maitland Werner, "President Chooses 20 as Members of Organized Crime Commission," *New York Times*, July 29, 1983.

17. Ronald J. Ostrow, "Reagan Picks Panel on Organized Crime," *Los Angeles Times*, July 29, 1983.

18. See, for example, Jack Anderson, "Feud over Turf May Jeopardize War on Crime," *Washington Post*, April 7, 1983.

7
Political Corruption in Small, Machine-Run Cities

David J. Bellis

T he lines dividing organized crime, politics, and corruption are difficult to draw clearly and impossible to define permanently. Nevertheless, the history and pattern of governmental law breaking by elected officials in some small cities demonstrates that corruption is more prevalent than commonly suspected. This analysis of small town political corruption and machine politics should contribute to our understanding of municipal corruption as a type of organized crime. Looking at corrupt small cities also alerts city watchers to the tactics used by some council members and other local officials to maintain their power illegally and benefit economically from governmental decision making.

This chapter focuses on election fraud, illegal zoning, nondisclosure of economic interests, and conflicts of interest by elected officials in small cities dominated by political machines and one or two powerful industries. Redevelopment of these cities to new uses after industry declines provides powerful incentives and opportunities for organized political corruption. Public resentment over this kind of corruption reveals itself in grass-roots citizen reform movements, in increasing contempt for politicians, and a belief that equal treatment under the law does not exist.

Election fraud is a form of organized municipal corruption with a long history in U.S. politics, particularly in machine-dominated cities. Southern blacks are no strangers to election fixing, the history of which led to amendment of the U.S. Constitution and federal voting rights legislation. Techniques used to fix elections include padding registration rolls, altering vote totals on tally sheets, actual ballot box stuffing, illegal registration and voting by nonresidents, illegal manipulation of the absentee voting process, voting in place of registered voters who have failed to vote, and intimidation of and actual physical assaults on voters (Steffens 1904; Asbury 1927; Landesco 1929; Royko 1971; Selvaggi 1978). Absentee voting is the latest trend, where political parties and candidates are engaged in an escalating race to see who can get the most voters to cast ballots in the comfort of their own homes. Voting by mail is also in use. Such techniques may increase turnout, but partisan third parties are walking out of peoples' homes with live absentee or mail-in ballots. This opens up the potential for ballot tampering.

Illegal zoning occurs in U.S. cities, especially those undergoing rapid physical development. Because the values at stake are enormous, it is not surprising that zoning is subject to heavy pressures by landowners and developers. Outright corruption is more than simply an occasional exception (U.S. National Commission on Urban Problems 1968: 19). In rapidly growing areas where old land uses are being given over to new ones, zoning decisions are likely to be the places where the most money is at stake, thus opening opportunities and powerful incentives for corruption. Further, building and construction codes are important to urban developers because they affect costs and are integral parts of corporate and development planning. Favorable construction regulations are as important as favorable property purchase arrangements provided through zoning. Such building and inspection ordinances and their administration are thus open to corruption.

Nondisclosure is the failure by public officials to disclose fully their economic interests in a jurisdiction, including real property, business partnerships or other corporate interests, gifts, loans, and outside employment. Disclosure laws seek to shed light on the outside interests of elected officials. They require routine reporting of situations that might suggest a conflict of interest. Disclosure laws open the private affairs of public officials to public scrutiny. Statements of economic interests filed by public officials should be monitored, analyzed, and investigated to control corruption opportunities.

Conflict of interest occurs when government officials improve their personal economic position by decisions they make in their official capacity. It is one-handed graft. The politician is at once the grantor of special favors and the beneficiary. Conflict of interest is a well-established common law principle based on the concept of a public office as a public, almost sacred trust. Although it is commonplace, conflict of interest is hard to prove. There is a vast gray area that shades the intersection between what is in the public interest and what is in an official's own private interest. Legal tests for conflict of interest are therefore extremely detailed and hard to prove. Nevertheless, there is widespread illegal use of public office for private gain without inducement or extortation of bribes. This is perhaps one of the most insidious forms of public corruption.

Some small cities contain all of these forms of organized political corruption. Such municipalities provide a laboratory in which to observe political corruption close up. The lines to power in these small cities are direct. The actors are easily identifiable, and their actions are unmistakably clear without the labyrinth of big-city politics.

Organized Crime and Political Corruption

The problem of organized crime in the United States is elusive in nature and difficult to define. Although legal definitions of it have been included in federal and state laws and working definitions have been adopted by government agencies, such definitions are limited in scope, designed to fulfill specific purposes. Other definitions are so broad and vague that they are virtually useless for analytical or investigative and prosecutorial purposes. Until the scope of organized crime activity, including organized political corruption, has been researched more thoroughly, a comprehensive definition of organized crime seems impossible.

Traditional definitions of organized crime focus on one or more of these categories:

1. The criminality of an illegal organization embodied in the law of conspiracy itself (Sutherland and Cressey 1955; U.S. National Advisory Committee on Criminal Justice Standards and Goals 1976: 215; R. Quinney 1979; Barlow 1981).
2. The syndicated supply of illegal goods and services, such as drugs, gambling, and prostitution (Asbury 1927; Landesco 1929; Albini 1971; Ianni and Reuss-Ianni 1977; Selvaggi 1978; Skolnick 1978; Anderson 1979; Bellis 1981).
3. Crimes relating to business activities, such as bankruptcy fraud, loan-sharking, extortion, bribery, racketeering, and false advertising and bunco schemes (Sutherland 1940a, 1940b, 1945, 1949, 1983; Clinard 1952; Geis and Meier 1977; Barlow 1981).
4. Traditional offenses such as theft and receiving stolen property when such offenses are organized and not strictly predatory crimes (Asbury 1927; Landesco 1929; Albini 1971; Selvaggi 1978).

5. Organized political corruption such as bribery of or extortion by
    public officials, conflict of interest, or perjury (Steffens 1904;
    Key 1936; Riordan 1963; Wilson 1963; Heidenheimer 1970; Gar-
    diner and Olson 1974; Amick 1976; Berg, Schmidhauser, and
    Hahn 1976; Geis and Meier 1977; Gardiner and Lyman 1978;
    U.S. National Advisory Committee on Criminal Justice Stan-
    dards and Goals, 1976).

This chapter focuses on the fifth category, crimes of political
corruption. Political corruption becomes organized crime when there
is corruption of public officials, violence or the threat of violence in
political communities, sophistication in the organization and commission of illegal political acts, continuity in terms of continual
illegal acts by public officials in the same community, and some
kind of structure under which the crimes are carried out, such as a
political machine.

When it comes to corruption of government officials, most traditional analyses approach the problem by way of criminals seeking
protection (bribery) or politicians extorting organized crime elements
for protection. The National Advisory Commission on Criminal Justice Standards and Goals (1973) stated that corruption of political
officials is particularly significant when perpetrated by organized
crime: "Of all the forms of illegal conduct in which organized crime
engages, official corruption is the most pernicious. . . . The vast
economic resources and strong-arm techniques available to organized crime are used to obtain favors and influence from public
officials" (p. 61).

The emergent concept is an epidemiologic one of organized crime
infecting a community like an outside contagion and corrupting local
officials to buy protection or local officials extorting crime figures
for payoffs. However, this traditional definition of political corruption—methods used by organized crime to protect its functionaries
against prosecution and/or convictions—does not always apply. In
some small cities, corruption among local elected officials and their
subordinate administrative employees is sui generis; they conspire
among themselves, perhaps in collusion with powerful private interests, to break the law. They might rig elections, illegally rezone
land, or engage in conflicts of interest. Such officials do not necessarily extort bribes for nonperformance of duties or take kickbacks
on contracts. Local elected officials can serve their own financial
and political interests without traditional organized crime elements
even being involved. Yet this is organized crime because in many
cases there is an actual conspiracy to engage in criminal acts, and it

is highly organized, though such conspiracies are extremely difficult to prove because of the sophistication of the perpetrators.

What Is Political Corruption?

In 1936, a general definition of political corruption was given as "the abuse of control over the power and resources of government for the purpose of personal or party profit" (Key 1936: 5). But it also includes "the nonlegal and illegal administration of government regulatory powers" (Gardiner and Olson 1974: 276). Heidenheimer thought it covered "misuse of authority as a result of considerations of personal gain, which need not be monetary" (Heidenheimer 1970: 3). Tammany Hall's boss, George Washington Plunkitt, said there was "dishonest graft" like theft and extortion by public officials and what he called "honest graft" like speculative land purchases in the path of future public construction right-of-ways: "They [the bosses] didn't steal a dollar from the city treasury. . . . There's an honest graft, and I'm an example of how it works. I might sum up the whole thing by sayin': I seen my opportunities and I took 'em" (quoted in Riordan 1963: 7).

Thus there seem to be at least three general types of illegal acts associated with political corruption. First is nonfeasance, failure by a public official to perform a required duty, "looking the other way." Second is malfeasance, the commission of some act by an official— like conflict of interest—that is positively unlawful. Third is misfeasance, the improper performance of some act that an official may otherwise properly do (Gardiner and Olson 1974: 113).

An important inducement to municipal corruption over the last one hundred years has been machine-style politics. Corrupt machine party organizations were built on the votes of newly arrived immigrants. Ethnic voters cast their ballots for machine candidates in return for favorable treatment and material rewards from the officials they helped elect. Machine bosses knew that what these disadvantaged urban dwellers wanted was help, not fancy anglicized versions of law and justice. The machines knew how to cut corners to provide that help. By distributing privileges, patronage, and other favors to their lower-class supporters, machine bosses organized electoral bases that allowed them to displace from political authority previously dominant Anglo Saxon politico-economic notables. Political corruption in machine cities became the cement that joined and fastened the otherwise separate and conflicting elements of ethnic neighborhoods and communities into a functioning body politic.

Some have noted, especially in foreign countries, that the results of governmental corruption need not necessarily be evil but rather functional. When bureaucracies are elaborate, inefficient, and staffed by human beings with foibles, the provision of strong incentives to bureaucrats to cut red tape may be the only way of speeding along a government decision (Leys 1965). In the United States the founding fathers purposefully designed a political system based on separation of powers and checks and balances. Because each branch and level of government can—and sometimes does—paralyze the other, some say that American government "is so constituted that it cannot be carried on without corruption" (Wilson 1966).

Corrupt cities seem to have their own life cycles of official misconduct bound to patterns of historical development. When cities were founded, the allocation of harbor and rail franchises created avenues of corruption. So did provision of police and fire services, two initial activities in which cities engage. Cities next usually develop the physical aspects of community: building streets, laying out water and sewer lines, constructing public buildings, providing extended transportation systems, and generally engaging in public works. Each of these activities requires land purchases and construction contracts that are vulnerable to bribes and kickbacks, self-dealing, and other abuses.

Rapid development in cities adds to the value of real estate and allows those with inside information to speculate in honest graft. Redevelopment in older cities where property is put to new uses is the latest fad, but it provides incentives and opens multiple opportunities for official corruption. The granting of leases and permits also opens expanded avenues for political corruption.

As cities grow in size, political corruption becomes more specialized. In small towns, the politically corrupt may be the very officials who themselves run the city. As cities mature and grow, organized political corruption becomes more specialized and differentiated so that the officials themselves may not even commit criminal acts. In some cities, campaign contributions—a form of legalized bribery—are sufficient to swing governmental decisions one way or the other in terms of benefiting special interests.

Along with physical development, cities adopt two kinds of regulations that are within their police power: legislation governing public morals (alcohol, prostitution, gambling) and those concerning physical development itself (zoning, permits, inspections). Nonenforcement or favorable enforcement of either type usually involves large-scale official corruption typified by conspiracies either to break or bend the law.

Research Methodology

The incidence and severity of political corruption in U.S. cities has not been studied systematically and in depth. Available information comes from newspaper exposés, personal accounts and biographies, case studies of particular cities, and impressionistic surveys of various time periods. The techniques employed to gather material for the examples presented in this chapter included research of official documentation from court records, analyses of appropriate statutes, and an examination of the results of investigations by law enforcement agencies. Property and business documentation has been collected and researched, including deeds, deeds of trust, quitclaim deeds, promissory notes, and official government permit documents. Other material was collected through surveys of newspaper reports and interviews with various public officials and ordinary citizens.

Perhaps most important in garnering material for this chapter has been participant observation. Our knowledge of the world is based principally on other people's observations, not on our own. Direct personal knowledge is our only means of ensuring that our theories are grounded on empirical fact. And when the heart of the observer is made to beat as the heart of any other member of the group under observation rather than as that of a detched emissary from some distant laboratory, then he or she has earned the title of participant observer (Madge 1965: 137). The primary task of participant observers is to enter into the life of the community being studied. If this task is achieved, there will be two consequences: their subjects will learn to take them for granted and thus behave almost as though they were not there, and they will learn to think almost as the subjects think.

In terms of participant observation for this research, for ten years I have led a grass-roots political reform movement in a small city ruled by a political machine. This nonintrusive observation allowed me, although an outspoken opponent of the city's power brokers, to watch them at close range and observe their behavior. Such observation including participating with them in actual governmental decision making as city councilman and redevelopment agency member since 1980 and most recently as mayor of the city. I have personally been involved in thirteen elections in the past seven years either as candidate or campaign manager, which allowed me an inside look at the electoral process in one small town. All of this experience has allowed me to penetrate a local political environment so that problems of corruption might be understood first hand, and not formulated with unnecessary personal, class, intellectual, or other bias or assumption.

Characteristics of Machine-Run Small Cities

Small cities dominated by one or two powerful business corporations and notable families often are conceived by their corporate and familial founders in self-protection, dedicated to the proposition that their municipalities should not be subject to outside rules or contaminated with things that the fief's leaders find offensive to their profit and personal sense of morality.

The glory years of such cities usually occur while industry is dominant, sometimes providing a lawless boom town atmosphere. Then, as transition occurs when traditional industries decay, community cleavages may appear over what kind of development will take place on land previously under industrial uses. While industry reigns, these corporations often assume nearly total control over local governmental regulation of their operations and of the city government itself. Often this seizure of political power by major corporations in small cities is accomplished in direct cooperation with local citizens who prosper and owe their livelihoods directly or indirectly to the dominant firms and their subsidiary service industries.

In small, corporate-controlled towns located in highly urbanized areas where there is a demand for new housing, when industrial operations decay and fade from the landscape, prime land is often freed up for residential and commercial-retail development. The main political cleavage in such cities is often over the quality, pace, and style of development. Local power elites tend to favor high-density, multifamily residential development, while grass-roots opposition forces demand lower-density zoning with building based on sensitive urban planning. Sometimes claims are made that local city council and other officials influence and vote on decisions that materially benefit their own property development interests in the city, as well as those of corporate landowners.

With industrial out-migration from these areas, open political control by dominant corporations is passed (often with corporate approval) to local politicians who tend to come from notable families and business backgrounds. Characteristically the elite families take over control of real estate, local politics, and the media. After industrial land uses recede, these families' property holdings can spread through a city rapidly, and they develop an interest in politics culminating in election of family members and supporters to city councils, leading to eventual control of a city's entire policymaking and administrative apparatus. A true political machine can develop; they are not necessarily structures of the past.

These political machines can be viewed as business organizations in a particular field of endeavor—getting votes and winning elections. Machines are hierarchical organizations run by bosses who depend on the allegiance of voters manipulated through patronage and other favors and who are reached at the block level by machine workers. Machines therefore depend on an informal exchange system of material incentives traded for votes to control elections and government.

Families associated with modern machine rule are often trusted, even revered by many local citizens. These local politicos gain political IOUs in classic small town ways: lending money to the poor, sending their family members over to help somebody put a roof on the house or pave a driveway, or fixing an elderly widow's toilet. They might even pay for the parts. And in politics it is axiomatic that a favor is always repaid with a favor. This is the essence of the political machine. At election time, the machine leaders call the citizens they helped and say, "Just callin' you. . . . Sure would like ya' to join us on election day." In this fashion, they take steps to secure their political and economic influence in a town.

Such elites often capture control of the local press to promulgate their own and corporate interests. They might buy a small town's only newspaper and purchase large blocks of subscriptions from its publisher. Such newspapers, in return for glowing articles about the ruling clan's service to the community and corporate operations in the city, can receive other windfalls, such as exclusive rights to publish the city's official notices and ordinances in the local paper.

In some machine-controlled cities, all council members ultimately can become part of the political machine, owing their election to the machine's street workers who get out the vote. Machine leaders hand pick polling place officials who count ballots and may allow open voting irregularities. Local machine thugs threaten recalcitrant voters into voting the "right" way. The machine picks the city manager, every department head, planning, civil service, and parks and recreation commissioners, and fills the ranks of subordinate civil service positions, including the police, with their own incompetent, often corrupt relatives, friends, and other cronies. Thus, politics in a small city can come to be dominated by a philistine hegemony of long-time city residents and business leaders, an old-boy network in which camaraderie, personal friendships, and outright corruption outweigh professionalism and textbook municipal administration. An organized pattern of vote rigging in electoins, questionable zoning practices, conflicts of interest, and even police misconduct may result.

Land booms often develop in small towns passing from an industrial phase into a residential and commercial development mode. Raw land and property formerly under heavy industrial uses goes into the hands of a select few real estate developers, some of whom may be city officials themselves, including council and planning commission members. New residential developments can spread over the city. The latest trend in these multifamily residential developments are condominiums for young home buyers unable to afford single-family houses and retired professional buyers who want to minimize the expense or effort of home upkeep. Such rapid development provides incentives and opportunities for official corruption in land use planning and zoning, as well as construction code development and enforcement.

Older industrial cities are often faced with unique situations with respect to land use planning and development. The majority of a city's land may have either been owned or had surface rights controlled by one or two industrial enterprises. When these industries decay or move out, there is a gradual release of land. Some of it is sold to private real estate developers. Or the previously dominant industrial concerns might become actively involved in real estate development themselves, perhaps spinning off a property development subsidiary, then buying prime land cheap under manufacturing zoning and seeing its value skyrocket when the zoning is changed to high-density residential or commercial.

City landscapes blighted by years of heavy industrial use are often red-lined by lenders. Nobody, especially the bankers, sees the land as being ripe for new uses. Cleanup of such blighted urban areas and provision of new public improvements like street, sewer, and water systems to support new uses today are being financed more frequently by urban redevelopment agencies. City councils establish these redevelopment agencies, draw their boundaries in broad swathes, taking in all undeveloped or blighted areas of the town, and often anoint themselves the redevelopment agency governing board. Then they usually rezone the so-called blighted land for new uses like high-density residential development.

City officials sell redevelopment as a way to finance public infrastructure to support new development. California State redevelopment law, for example, provides that tax increments from increased valuation provided by new development in blighted redevelopment areas may be used to finance this kind of infrastructure and public service improvements, as well as to acquire land, and to carry out the purposes of a city's redevelopment plan. Redevelopment provides yet another series of incentives for official misconduct, especially in corrupt, machine-controlled cities.

Typically with redevelopment, controversy ensues during which classic opposing interests can split sharply. If developers dominate city politics, they usually want high-density zoning in at least part of the redevelopment areas so they can milk the housing market. Residentially zoned vacant land in a city can be exploited for quick profit, a good deal of which may even accrue to some city council members themselves who are real estate developers in their jurisdictions. The antidevelopment faction usually wants more planning options, more controlled, lower-density development, often referred to as growth management.

When local officials with property holdings and development interests in redevelopment project areas sit on redevelopment agency governing boards, there is potential for organized political corruption. Almost all redevelopment agency decisions bring improvements to a city that serve new development. While the idea of redevelopment, with its tax increments to finance public infrastructure, is theoretically sound, it can provide further incentives and opportunities for council people who double as redevelopment agency members and who buy land and build commercially in redevelopment areas to dip into the public trough.

Further, city council and redevelopment agency members who are building contractors and/or real estate developers in their cities must obtain construction permits from their own building departments, as well as city inspections and approvals for their projects. In small cities, building and planning departments usually have only a few employees who review plans and construction activities. Since the compensation, promotion, and discipline of these employees is subject to review and sometimes direct approval by elected officials, there is at least the appearance of impropriety, if not outright corruption, when developer-council members have their own development activities subject to review and approval by the very building and planning department over which they have direct control. It is not uncommon to see conspiracies to break the law between such elected officials and their own departmental employees. Such employees will dance to the tune of their political superiors either because their jobs are on the line or they are paid off with other material incentives.

Redevelopment in a small city also can benefit the dominant

corporations since they often own a great deal of property in designated redevelopment areas. The value of their property can be dramatically increased by and its development potential escalated as a result of public improvements put in by redevelopment agencies or zoning changes.

For the small elite groups who run these machine cities, there is some pleasure in seeing dirty industry leave and new development go in. But in order to maintain their dominance, such machines embark on a political course where municipal boundaries of closet size create opportunities for organized crimes like election fraud, illegal zoning, nondisclosure by public officials of their economic interests, and felony conflicts of interest.

Voting Fraud in Machine Cities

In some cities, almost every municipal election is conducted under the cloud of election fraud charges. Despite their lopsided political superiority over local opposition, political machines never fail to run scared. For this reason, or perhaps out of habit, they never miss a chance to steal a certain number of votes and trample the voting laws. They get away with it because city clerks and voting precinct judges never protest and citizens are not well organized enough to root out the illegal practices. Allegations, when they are made, usually include actual ballot box stuffing; nonresidents, such as business people or machine-controlled voters, being illegally registered and illegally voting; death threats and physical intimidation of voters by machine thugs; registering and voting by incompetent voters in community care facilities like nursing homes and mental institutions; and election officials like city clerks or partisan third parties campaigning for machine candidates and ballot issues in voters' homes while they mark their absentee ballots and then walking away with the live ballots.

Chicago has come in for the lion's share of voter fraud corruption. Prior to Harold Washington's election in 1983, for example, voting officials took pictures of twenty-two of 6,000 allegedly bogus addresses of registered voters. Those twenty-two included boarded up-buildings, a McDonald's restaurant, and a tree in Chicago's Humboldt Park *(Long Beach Press-Telegram*, February 23, 1983).

The commonplace in Chicago is believed to be impossible in cleaner cities out West, for example, where the closest thing to an election scandal is usually an occasional dispute over the true residence of a candidate, not the residence—or even existence—of the people who vote for the candidate. But in at least some cities, even in southern California, nonresident voting is commonplace and, as in Chicago, in elections the headquarters address of the local machine's campaign committee might well be the local cemetery. Indeed the conduct of municipal elections in some machine-run small towns in California resembles that in Chicago.

A number of well-orchestrated acts can corrupt the voting process to fix an election. A city clerk might personally deliver ballots to absentee voters and then carry them back to city hall. This is legal, but citizens in some cities allege that their city clerk campaigns for machine candidates or helps those absentee voters mark their ballots for the "right" candidates.

Citizens have testified that they have seen city clerks sign elderly nursing home patients' absentee ballots in municipal elections. They assert that certain council candidates sometimes accompany clerks to nursing homes to get these elderly patients' votes. The clerks might also mark the ballots for the elderly. Thus it is possible that machine candidates can garner over 60 percent of all absentee voters in a municipal election—many of them from nursing home patients—while none of the opposition can gain more than 10 percent of the absentee vote. The administrator of one nursing home who was involved in such an election has complained:

> [The city clerk] and his staff came to our Convalescent Hospital for the purpose of obtaining the absentee ballots from the voters they had registered. [He] used very inappropriate means of gathering these votes from the patients. . . . Members of my staff heard the above mentioned persons telling the voters who and what to vote for. I feel this completely violated the rights of the voters to their freedom of choice. I also feel that some of the people [the clerk] registered were incompetent of understanding what they were, in fact, voting for.[1]

Two years later, the same kind of irregularities occurred at the same nursing home in another municipal election. This repeated hustling of senile absentee voters by the city clerk and other machine street workers prompted a request from the convalescent hospital administrator that in the future, "all Absentee Ballots for any patient. . . . be sent to them through the mail. . . . In this manner we feel that any voting that is done by the patients will be done on their own through their own convictions."[2]

City clerks might illegally allow some absent voters to violate absentee voter application time limits specified in the California

Elections Code: "Application for an absent voter's ballot shall be made in writing to the elections official having jurisdiction over the election between the 29th and 7th day prior to the election" (California State Elections Code, sec. 1002)." One absentee voter testified she asked for her absentee ballot just three days before a municipal election and got it. It was personally delivered to her by the city clerk who then proceeded illegally to campaign in her living room by telling her how to vote while she was marking her absentee ballot.

Political machines use the absentee voting process to tip close elections in their favor. In a small town where only 1,000 or so voters turn out, 150 absentee votes can control electoral outcomes. Absentee vote counts in machine cities may not reflect regular precinct vote tallies. The absentee count can heavily favor machine-backed candidates. Table 7.1 presents the results from three municipal elections in a small, machine-run city.

It is also common in machine cities to allow nonresidents to vote. Machine election workers can register phony voters at safe addresses in the city and then march them in on election day to cast their ballots. Or business people who are nonresidents will register and vote using their business addresses. Some business people see

Table 7–1
Election Results Comparing Machine and Nonmachine Candidates in Absentee and Regular Precinct Vote Tallies

	Absentee Votes	*Total Votes*
1978 municipal election		
Nonmachine candidate	9 (6%)	171
Nonmachine candidate	6 (4%)	159
Nonmachine candidate	9 (6%)	342
Machine candidate	58 (36%)	386 (Winner)
Machine candidate	62 (38%)	398 (Winner)
Nonmachine candidate	12 (6%)	200
Nonmachine candidate	6 (4%)	201
1980 municipal election		
Nonmachine candidate	12 (6%)	569 (Winner)
Machine candidate	56 (29%)	536 (Winner)
Machine candidate	21 (11%)	492 (Winner)
Nonmachine candidate	15 (7%)	426
Machine candidate	43 (22%)	390
Machine candidate	49 (25%)	377
1981 recall of Nonmachine candidate		
Total vote cast: Yes on recall = 458 votes (37%)		
No on recall = 622 votes (63%)		
Total absentee: Yes on recall = 109 votes (82%)		
No on recall = 25 votes (18%)		

Source: Municipal voting statistics from 1978, 1980, and 1981 elections.

nothing wrong with this. They believe that because they work and pay taxes in a city, they have a right to participate in the selection of municipal elected officials whose policies affect the business community. Other nonresident business persons who vote, however, clearly know that voting is illegal if they do not live in a city, but they are part of an organized effort to swing elections illegally.

Threats and physical intimidation of voters can be carried out by thugs under orders from the machine. A voter who owns a small business in a machine city has related that during an election, she was told by a machine spokesperson to take an opposition candidate's sign out of her business window. "You'll be dead in this town," he told her, if she did not remove the sign. "What do you mean, 'dead' in this town," she asked? He said, "We could have you blown away." A frightened, single woman, she took down the sign.

Typically threats are directed to voters who are easily intimidated. Another woman in a machine city, elderly and living alone, said that minutes after putting a nonmachine candidate's sign in her living room window, she received an anonymous telephone threat that if the sign was not taken down she would get a fire bomb through her window. She immediately removed the sign.

The lives of nonmachine candidates have been threatened by machine enforcers. The day after one such candidate openly alleged felony conflict of interest against a machine mayor, his wife's eighty-seven-year-old wheelchair-bound grandmother got an anonymous telephone call: "Tell your granddaughter to stop what she's doing [investigating corruption in this city] or I'll take what I have in my hand, shove it up her nose and blow her brains out."[3] These scare tactics work with some would-be citizen watchdogs, and scare them away from their constitutionally protected right of political participation.

Election day in some machine-run small cities can see the campaign signs of machine-sponsored candidates nailed adjacent to polling places, in violation of the California Elections Code, which outlaws such campaign advertising within 100 feet of any polling place. Police cars might park in front of polling places, blocking entrances, with their red lights flashing in attempts to intimidate voters away from the polls. Poll watchers routinely assigned by nonmachine opposition candidates to check for irregularities are sometimes threatened and thrown out of polling places if they assert their right to observe the balloting process, especially the counting of votes.

In substance, these organized illegal tactics can and do ensure election victories for a political machine's hand-picked candidates for city council, city clerk, city treasurer, and local initiatives, referenda, and recalls. In this fashion, corrupt political machines seek to maintain their grip over the policymaking and administrative machinery of a city. This becomes organized crime when conspiracies exist to plan and carry out these acts of election fixing. Correcting the problem is difficult when local election officials are hit with hundreds of complaints during election campaigns that are difficult to investigate and prosecute with limited resources.

Illegal Zoning

Major land development usually requires zoning decisions. Zoning originated in the United States with a rather limited purpose: to prevent the development of incompatible uses in adjoining areas. As the concept of urban planning evolved in the early twentieth century, regulatory tools became proactive devices to shape growth management as well as environmental issues. Going beyond the exclusion of specific unpopular land uses, planning, zoning, and other devices began to be used to allocate land uses for future types of development (Babcock 1966; Mandelker 1971).

In zoning, those who win often gain increased property values or more lucrative business income. The losers may suffer lower property values, business failure, or general dissatisfaction with the quality of development in a city (Hinds, Carn, and Ordway 1979: 1). It is not surprising, then, that "in some communities there is a very real problem of corruption in zoning decisions" (National Commission on Urban Problems, 1968: 19). The value of property is strongly tied to its zoning classification. Land zoned for high-density residential development, for example, is usually worth many times the value of land zoned for single-family housing or manufacturing use (Gardiner and Lyman 1978: 52).

Major small town property owners like dominant industrial concerns and certain developer-councilmen and redevelopment agency members may find that their land, when rezoned to allow high-density residential development, is worth many times more than it would have been under manufacturing or lower-density residential zoning designations. It is not surprising that the zoning system is subject to enormous pressures by public officials, landowners, and developers and that outright corruption occurs frequently. Sometimes there are well-planned conspiracies among elected officials, their subordinate planning and zoning staffs, and private sector interests to rezone property illegally. Such illegalities might include failure to properly notice or hold public hearings on zoning changes, spot zoning, or illegally overturning voter-ordered zoning decisions that result from initiatives and referenda.

Those who control zoning decisions control land values. If real estate developers control a majority of votes on a five-member city council, the council might surreptitiously, and without required public hearings, overturn the results of a low-density voter referendum and reinstall their previously approved high-density zoning designations in residentially zoned areas. This could open the way for development of massive, high-density condominium complexes that a majority of voters vetoed in the referendum election. As a result of this kind of illegal zoning, land values can shoot from under $2 a square foot to over $60 a square foot. Those who buy cheap under previous manufacturing or low-density residential zoning are the big financial winners. Voters, who might want to keep down population growth and retain a small town atmosphere, are the losers.

Legally, a city's official zoning map and zoning code text, taken together, constitute its zoning code (Gardiner and Lyman 1978: 16). When such a code is being adopted or amended, separate public hearings must be publicly noticed and held by a planning commission and city council on both the proposed text and map change (California Government Code, sec. 65854).

Long-time city residents who want to hold down population growth might object to a newly adoped high-density zoning code. They could walk door to door gathering signatures necessary to put the new code to a referendum vote so voters themselves might determine whether they want high or low-density residential zoning If such a referendum is approved, it vetos the new zoning code and has the legal effect of requiring the city to go back immediately to the zoning that was in place before the new code was adopted. It is a direct, legal order from voters for lower-density zoning and development. But if the city council is dominated by a builder majority, they could illegally bypass the low-density requirement established by voters and slip back in the defeated high-density zoning map and return to the old low-density zoning code text. This action by a council would effectively double-cross voters by ignoring the referendum result. It would circumvent the referendum by illegally adopting the high-density official zoning map in an ordinance defeated by the voters.

Citizens might then claim that all new development is actually illegal because of this conspiracy to rezone land to benefit major landowners, some of whom may actually be on the city council. Charges of conflict of interest will be made and allegations submitted to the district attorney's office, which may or may not investigate them. But the goal of the pro-growth forces is usually accomplished: the city's zoning is illlegally changed to serve developers, contrary to the wishes of the electorate.

Such cases might involve actual conspiracies to circumvent the law among elected council members, subordinate planning and zoning staff, and private landowners and developers. Thus, this can be organized crime as well, but criminality is extremely difficult to prove because the perpetrators are well schooled at covering their tracks. Citizens often do not know where to begin such an investigation.

Nondisclosure of Economic Interests by City Council Members

Some city council members may conceal their own multiple property holdings and other business interests in the jurisdiction within which they serve, especially if political power is firmly in the hands of a corrupt machine and disclosure statements are not carefully scrutinized by city watchdogs. If these council members are accused of corruption, they usually maintain their innocence. They claim they have fully disclosed their property interests and business deals in the city and have never misused their official position.

Some city council and redevelopment agency members who are real estate developers may be engaged in various development projects in their own cities. This is why in California they must file an initial statement of economic interests within thirty days of their election to office and an annual statement of economic interests every year thereafter while they hold office (California Government Code, sec. 87202, 87203).

In some cases, when citizens investigate these economic disclosure statements of developers on city councils and redevelopment agency governing boards, they find glaring discrepancies between what the officials report on their initial and annual statements and their actual property holdings and other business investments. What often emerges is an intricate web of possible violations, many interwoven and touching several areas of state conflict-of-interest laws. Alleged nondisclosure is often one facet. These charges are difficult to prove since these politicians' activities are often marked by a dizzying panoply of quitclaiming, complex partnership agreements, and submerged interests that are covered to hide thier interests from public scrutiny. There are warranty deeds, deeds of trust, joint tenancy grant deeds, grant deeds, assignments of deeds of trust, quit-claims, and other promissory notes that make these cases extremely complex and difficult to unravel, even for the most experienced investigators. Nonetheless, in some cities, watchdog citizen groups have discovered abundant documentation of nondisclosure of economic interests by city council and redevelopment agency members.

One councilman-developer in a small machine-run city failed to disclose four of his business partnerships organized to purchase land and develop multifamily residential projects in the town's redevelopment area. He was also a redevelopment agency member. After investigating the charge that the councilman's business partnerships were undisclosed, the city attorney concluded: "[The councilman's] interest was substantial enough under the provisions of the Political Reform Act to require that he disclose these investments . . . we think the better practice would have been [for him] to report the partnerships on the disclosure statements." The city attorney said that each of this councilman's undisclosed partnerships "should have [been] included on initial and annual statements of economic interest." But he let the councilman off the hook, concluding that his nondisclosures were not "deliberate" and that "any errors which [he] made have been made inadvertently and in good faith."[4] As it turned out, the undisclosed partnerships were organized to buy land in the city and to finance, seek city approval for, and construct condominium projects in the city redevelopment area. As councilman, this elected official also served as a governing member of the city's redevelopment agency, formed to finance new street, sewer, and water system improvements to support new condominium development in the town.

California redevelopment law precludes redevelopment agency members from buying property in their city's redevelopment areas:

> No agency or community officer or employee who in the course of his duties is required to participate in the formulation of or to approve the plans and policies for the redevelopment of a project area shall acquire interest in any property included within a project area within the community. If any such officer or employee owns or has any direct or indirect financial interest in such property he shall immediately make a written disclosure of it to the Agency. . . . Failure to so disclose constitutes misconduct in office. (California Government Code, sec. 33130)

The law is specific regarding redevelopment agency members who would purchase property in redevelopment areas. The code was designed to prohibit any agency member from acquiring property in redevelopment areas because almost every decision an agency member makes could benefit these investments and he or she might use public largesse for private gain.

Notably, escrow closed on two of this councilman's redevelopment area property acquisitions after his election to the council and redevelopment agency. Further, he had also purchased a lot of redevelopment area property as a planning commissioner where he served for two years, having been appointed by the council's machine-dominated majority who was grooming him for the city council. Redevelopment area property purchases by redevelopment agency members are clearly illegal. But what about redevelopment area property acquisitions by planning commissioners? Do they violate California Government Code section 33130? It would seem that a planning commissioner is a community officer ivnolved with decision-making powers concerning a city's blighted areas. That a planning commissioner is such an officer is indicated by California Government Code sections 33325, 33330, 33346, and 33347, all of which make the city planning commission's role mandatory in local redevelopment policymaking.

This council member also failed to disclose twenty-one separate parcels of property he owned in the city. The California Political Reform Act of 1974 requires office-holders to disclose interests in real property valued at over $1,000 within the jurisdiction in which they serve. Such property must be disclosed on both initial and annual statements of economic interests. This councilman's nondisclosed property holdings were intimately tied to his unreported business partnerships because the partnerships were organized to develop condominium projects on the unreported land. Some of his twenty-one undisclosed lots were purchased through his concealed partnerships. For example, one of the nondisclosed partnerships owned fourteen of the unreported lots, another five of the hidden lots and a third, two of the lots. Said the city attorney:

> From our review of [the councilman's] affidavit, it would appear that his interest in each of the above-named partnerships is sufficient so that all the above-named parcels would be reportable as interests in real property owned by business entities in which [the councilman] has greater than 10% share. . . . We conclude that all 21 parcels were reportable.[5]

Although the council-appointed city attorney confirmed discrepancies and omissions in the councilman's statements of economic interests, he ruled the statements could be amended to correct them; however, even after the city attorney gave him a chance to amend the statements, the councilman still failed to disclose four parcels owned by his undisclosed partnerships.

Citizen watchdog groups that suspect nondisclosure should always compare their elected officials' statements of economic interests to county property tax rolls and other sources to determine whether the officials are fully disclosing their investments. The organized crime aspect of nondisclosure is that the decision by an elected official not to disclose business interests fully is one that might be made in concert with his or her development partners out of government. When their councilman-partner is charged with nondisclosure, such outside business associates almost never stand up to set the record straight in terms of their financial relationship to the elected official.

Felony Conflicts of Interst by City Council– Redevelopment Agency Members

Felony conflict of interest is defined in California Government Code section 87100: "No public official at any level of state or local government shall make, participate in making, or in any way attempt to use his official position to influence a governmental decision in which he knows or has reason to know he has a financial interest." The California Fair Political Practices Commission (FPPC) has set forth a difficult-to-prove test for determining whether a public official has a financial interest in a decision and therefore must abstain:

> Under [California Government Code section 87100] several elements must be present before a public official is required to disqualify himself from participation in a governmental decision. First, it must be reasonably foreseeable that the governmental decision will have a financial effect. Second, the anticipated financial effect must be on a financial interest of the official. . . . Third, the anticipated financial effect must be material. Fourth, the governmental decision's anticipated financial effect on the official's financial interest must be distinguishable from its effect on the public generally. *(In the Matter of Thorner, 1976, 1 F.P.P.C. Ops. 198, 202)*

Thus an elected official must disqualify himself or herself from participating in a governmental decision where: (1) he or she has an existing, legally recognized interest in real property; (2) which may foreseeably be materially financially affected by his decision; (3) in a fashion distinguishable from the decision's effect on the public generally.

One local councilman–redevelopment agency member acquired a one-half interest in a 2¼-acre commercially zoned parcel in the city's redevelopment area. He eventually sold the site for $745,000 (his one-half interest share was $372,000) to a developer who built a fifty-six-unit condominium complex on it. Although it was only approved for forty-eight units by the planning commission and city council, the ultimate developer got permission from the city's planning director to jump to fifty-six units.

There were two problems to development of this property: the property was commercially zoned, precluding residential development, and it had no street bordering it from which to take required access. It was alleged that the councilman solved both problems, in violation of California Government Code section 87100, through his official votes and other actions as council and redevelopment agency member. These decisions allegedly increased his profit from the final sale of the property to its ultimate developer.

This councilman's first problem—that of the property's commercial zoning designation—arose from the fact that by ordinance, the city had set aside certain commercial land along major streets as commercial zoning. This was designed to keep residential development from encroaching on land reserved for retail sales tax-generating businesses to shore up the city's tax base (most California cities get about half their revenue from sales taxes returned by the state). While one of his relatives still owned this 2¼-acre commercial parcel, the official voted on council to open up this commercially zoned property to residential development. A month after his vote and with the property now legally zoned for more profitable multifamily condominium development, the relative deeded ownership in the land over to him.

Critics argued that he had a material financial interest in this vote, even though at the time the property was not legally his. They alleged it was "too close for comfort," arguing either that he was acting as his relative's agent in voting or that he would end up with the property himself, which he did a month later.

This councilman–redevelopment agency member also participated in a specially called redevelopment agency meeting where the agency appropriated over $400,000 and awarded a contract for construction of a new public street bordering and providing required vehicular access to and from the same 2¼-acre parcel. By this time,

he claimed he had sold the property, however. Redevelopment conflict-of-interest law specifically prohibits specifically prohibits agency
officers from wielding influence on decisions affecting their own
financial interests in real property.

Another issue associated with cities undergoing rapid development is regulation of construction site noise. Residents living next
to large construction projects, for example, might demand no week-
end construction and none before 7 A.M. and after 7 P.M., along
with strict police enforcement of the ordinance. This same councilman voted down a tougher noise control ordinance. Did he want
to ensure that the city's noise regulations did not hinder construction
on property in which he had a financial interest? Might he materially
benefit by building at night and on weekends?

He also may have engaged in a conflict of interest when he voted
against a zoning code amendment to tighten the city's density standards. The amendment reduced density by increasing the amount of
lot space required per each condominium unit from 1,350 square
feet per unit to 1,750 square feet per unit, thus permitting fewer
units per lot. This more restrictive density standard affected the
councilman's own one-half interest in the same 2¼-acre commercially zoned parcel. The more restrictive ordinance amendment would
have cut his project on this site from the originally proposed forty-
eight units to thirty-six units. His estimated financial interest in
this decision was a possible $600,000 loss, based on potentially twelve
fewer units at a conservative $100,000 each (based on his one-half
interest in the property). In voting no to lower density at the council
meeting, this councilman said, "Hey, there's nothing wrong with
the [higher-density] ordinance we already have. This [new] ordinance
is too restrictive and it's going to curtail progress."[6] At the same
council meeting, this council member lobbied and voted to defeat
another zoning code amendment that would have prohibited so-
called tandem parking in new condominium developments. In this
method, one car is allowed to be parked behind the other in one's
condominium garage or required outdoor parking space. It increases
density by cutting driveway turn-around space from twenty-five to
twelve feet, thus giving developers more room to add dwelling units.
The city attorney advised this councilman not to vote on these decisions, but he did.

Another of this same official's votes on council in which he may
have had a financial interest and from which he may have benefited
economically was a new ordinance amendment requiring off-street

guest parking spaces in new condominium complexes. The tough new off-street guest parking rule died on council when this official voted no. No required off-street guest parking meant developers could build more units on a lot. This councilman had just sold his 2¼-acre site at the time of this vote.

This councilman—redevelopment agency member cast a number of other votes from which citizens alleged he derived financial benefits. Is this kind of conflict of interest organized crime? It is when it is a continuing, conspiratorial, well-structured enterprise involving elected officials, their subordinate staff, and private developers. It is when a pattern of this kind of activity exists in a small town controlled by a political machine and a few dominant corporations and land developers. Conflict of interest like this is rampant; together it constitutes millions of dollars every year stolen out of taxpayers' pockets.

Conclusion: What Is to Be Done?

The business of America is business. The governmental ruling arms of a business-dominated society are loathe to intimidate the metabolism of money making, especially their own, with nagging matters of illegalities, proper planning, and the public interest. Why should developers on a city council and redevelopment agency governing board, for example, rush to impose tough regulations on the building industries? They are just doing their jobs as representatives and participants in this business. The rub is that they also are entrusted by the public to represent everybody's interests, not just their own and those of their partner-builders out of government.

Laws are on the books to prevent, detect, and prosecute organized political corruption, but little seems to be done about it. These laws are complex and set extremely high standards of proof. In terms of self-correction from inside government itself, if citizens leave the job of preventing, detecting, and correcting political corruption to local officials they pay to run their government, they run the risk of nothing being done, especially if the local officials themselves are tainted. State and local laws regarding conflicts of interest, financial disclosure, declaration of interests, open meetings and records, and codes of ethics seek to set down in formal fashion what a community expects of its public officials and public employees. But such statutes are easily broken or bent, and outside investigation is almost always necessary to uncover official lawbreaking.

What about investigations of official corruption from the outside by citizen watchdog groups? There are several reasons why citizens often fail to prove their cases against corrupt public officials. First, citizen information on political corruption is often only as good as what appears in the local press. Big-city broadcast and print media are notorious for neglecting political corruption, especially in outlying smaller communities. This creates a news vacuum. Newspapers in the suburban small towns themselves may be controlled by local elites who are part of a corrupt political machine. Thus, they print nothing that maligns local political and economic notables. And the public's ability to know about corruption from the media is severely restricted.

Second, if the media pay little attention to corruption in government and watchdog groups take on investigations themselves, they are severely hampered because many such groups lack even the most basic investigative skills to uncover and prove local political corruption.

A corruption investigation carried on by unskilled volunteers rarely succeeds. To be effective, these groups need independent funding, permanent investigative staff, including legal assistance, and close relations with cooperative news media. These resources are often lacking, so watchdog groups find it extremely difficult to sustain long-term, effective investigative operations.

Third, some citizen groups like Chicago's Better Government Association (BGA), the many chapters of the League of Women Voters, Santa Monica, California's Campaign for Economic Democracy, and other narrowly based municipal taxpayer groups have had some success. But their focus is most often on objective analyses of issues, electing candidates to office or pushing single issues like rent control, or advocacy of cost reductions in government (most taxpayer groups). They do not really focus on municipal corruption.

Further, citizen watchdog groups sometimes take on partisan tones when they fight city hall. When they do, they lose credibility with the public, the media, and even their own constituents. And civic leaders and the media often view the public exposure of corruption as an attack on the economic health of the community or simply an attempt by the protesters to substitute a new set of rascals for the current one. Citizens on the attack often find that they themselves become targets of contempt, ridicule, or even libel suits brought against them by accused politicians and business people who are implicated in political corruption schemes. A $10 million libel action against a group of neighbors can quickly chill their enthusiasm for going after corruption.

In the end, there is a feeling of helplessness. If all forms of organized crime are added together, including corporate and political crime, one begins to suspect that organized crime runs the country and is such an integral part of the political, economic, and social fabric that it will never be obliterated. The public today takes for granted that crooks are involved in just about every major enterprise in the country. People are numb, acceptant, and withdrawn. In this post-Watergate era, political corruption is viewed as merely an extension or refinement of earlier illegal and unethical practices in U.S. government. Corruption is politics as usual. It seems as if there is no justice, that the whole world is taking advantage of the opportunities and incentives for organized crime.

Are there solutions? Not until federal, state, and local elected officials and prosecutorial agencies give as much emphasis to governmental and corporate crime as they do to street crime, huge cocaine busts, undercover marijuana buys on high schools campuses, and the like will political corruption be affected. The public will have to push them to do this. Under our current value system, the rewards for going after organized crime, including political corruption, do not measure up to strokes received by politicians and law enforcement when they pursue street crime—crimes, by the way, with a higher probability of conviction than organized crime.

Politicians and prosecutors give white-collar organized crime, especially political corruption, short shrift. It is a pandora's box that if opened would drain law enforcement resources away from those crimes like burglary and drug law violations that their bosses—elected officials—and the public seem to want crushed at all cost.

Notes

1. Personal letter from nursing home administrator to the author, June 6, 1976.
2. Personal letter to the author from nursing home administrator, July 16, 1978.
3. Transcript of telephone conversation.
4. City Attorney report to a California city council, November 6, 1980.
5. City Attorney report to a California city council, November 6, 1980.
6. City Council minutes, February 6, 1978.

References

Albini, Joseph L. 1971. *The American Mafia: Genesis of a Legend.* New York: Appleton, Century-Crofts.

Amick, George. 1975. *The American Way of Graft.* Princeton: Center for Analysis of Public Issues.

Anderson, Annelise G. 1979. *The Business of Organized Crime: A Cosa Nostra Family.* Stanford, Calif.: Hoover Institution Press.

Asbury, Herbert. 1927. *The Gangs of New York: An Informal History of the Underworld.* New York: Alfred A. Knopf.

Babcock, Richard. 1966. *The Zoning Game: Municipal Practices and Politics.* Madison: University of Wisconsin Press.

Barlow, Hugh D. 1981. *Introduction to Criminology.* 2d ed. Boston: Little, Brown.

Bellis, David J. 1981. *Heroin and Politicians: The Failure of Public Policy to Control Addition in America.* Westport, Conn.: Greenwood Press.

Berg, Larry; John Schmidhauser; and Harlan Hahn. 1976. *Corruption in the American Political System.* Morristown, N.J.: General Learning Press.

Clinard, Marshall. 1952. *The Black Market.* New York: Holt, Rinehart and Winston.

Gardiner, John A., and Theodore R. Lyman. 1978. *Decisions for Sale: Corruption and Reform in Land-Use and Building.* New York: Praeger Publishers.

————, and David J. Olson, eds. 1974. *Theft of the City: Readings on Corruption in Urban America.* Bloomington: Indiana University Press.

Geis, Gilbert, and Robert F. Meier, eds. 1977. *White-Collar Crime: Offenses in Business, Politics, and the Professions.* Rev. ed. New York: Free Press.

Heidenheimer, Arnold J., ed. 1970. *Political Corruption: Readings in Comparative Analysis.* New York: Holt, Rinehart and Winston.

Hinds, Dudley S.; Neil G. Carn; and O. Nicholas Ordway. 1979. *Winning at Zoning.* New York: McGraw-Hill.

Ianni, Francis A.J., and Elizabeth Reuss-Ianni. 1977. *The Crime Society: Organized Crime and Corruption in America.* New York: New American Library.

Key, V.O., Jr. 1936. "The Techniques of Political Graft in the United States." Ph.D. dissertation, University of Chicago.

Landesco, John. 1929. *Organized Crime in Chicago.* Chicago: University of Chicago Press.

Leys, Colin. 1965. "What Is the Problem about Corruption?" *Journal of Modern African Studies* 2 (August): 217–224.

Long Beach Press-Telegram, February 23, 1983.

Madge, John. 1965. *The Tools of Social Science: An Analytical Description of Social Science Techniques.* Garden City, N.Y.: Doubleday.

Mandelker, Daniel R. 1971. *The Zoning Dilemma: A Legal Strategy for Urban Change.* Indianapolis: Bobbs-Merrill.

Quinney, Earl R. 1964. "The Study of White Collar Crime: Toward a Reorientation in Theory and Research." *Journal of Criminal Law, Criminology and Police Science* 55 (June): 208–214.

Quinney, Richard. 1979. *Criminology.* 2d ed. Boston: Little, Brown.

Riordan, William R. 1963. *Plunkitt of Tammany Hall.* New York: E.P. Dutton and Company.

Royko, Mike. 1971. *Boss: Richard J. Daley of Chicago.* New York: New American Library.

Selvaggi, Guiseppe. 1978. *The Rise of the Mafia in New York: From 1896 through World War II.* Translated and edited by William A. Packer. Indianapolis: Bobbs-Merrill.

Skolnick, Jerome. 1978. *House of Cards.* Boston: Little, Brown.

Steffens, Lincoln. 1904. *The Shame of the Cities.* New York: McClure, Phillips and Company.

Sutherland, Edwin H. 1940a. "White-Collar Criminality." *American Sociological Review* 5 (February): 1–12.

———. 1940b. "Crime and Business." *Annals of the American Academy of Political and Social Science* 217 (September): 112–118.

———. 1945. "Is 'White-Collar Crime' Crime?" *American Sociological Review* 10 (April): 132–139.

———. 1949. *White Collar Crime.* New York: Dryden Press.

———. 1983. *White Collar Crime: The Uncut Version.* New Haven: Yale University Press.

———, and Donald R. Cressey. 1955. *Principles of Criminology.* 3d ed. New York: J.B. Lippincott.

U.S. Government. 1973. National Advisory Commission on Criminal Justice Standards and Goals. "Community Crime Prevention." Washington, D.C.: Government Printing Office.

———. 1976. National Advisory Commission on Criminal Justice Standards and Goals. "Organized Crime: Report of the Task Force on Organized Crime." Washington, D.C.: Government Printing Office.

———. 1968. National Commission on Urban Problems. Final Report. "Building the American City." Washington, D.C.: Government Printing Office.

Wilson, James Q. 1963. "The Police and Their Problems: A Theory." *Public Policy* 12 (Winter): 190–199.

———. 1966. "Corruption: The Shame of the States." *Public Interest* 2 (Winter): 30–35.

8

Asset Forfeiture under the Federal Criminal Law

G. Robert Blakey

> [RICO] attacks the problem by providing a means of wholesale removal of organized crime from our organizations, prevention of their return and, where possible, forfeiture of their ill-gotten gains.
>
> Senator John L. McClellan
> 116 Cong. Rec. 591 (1970)

In 1970, Congress enacted two statutes that marked a sharp break with the past. In the Racketeer Influenced and Corrupt Organizations (RICO) provisions of Title IX of the Organized Crime Control Act[1] and the Continuing Criminal Enterprise (CCE) provisions of Title II of the Comprehensive Drug Abuse Prevention and Control Act of 1970,[2] Congress reestablished a form of asset forfeiture that had not been utilized since the Civil War.[3] Most of the legislation enacted in the post–Civil War period had provided for civil forfeiture. In the 1970 acts, Congress authorized criminal forfeiture. Congress's purpose in enacting these statutes was to curtail the profits of criminal endeavors as well as sever the connection between offenders and their bases of economic power. Little of that has happened since 1970 undercuts the legitimacy of Congress's concern with the danger to free institutions posed by a generation of illicit income. The annual flow of illicit funds in the area of drugs is thought to be more than $79 billion.[4] The annual flow of illicit funds in the area of theft and fencing may be as high as $40 billion.[5] And the annual flow of illicit funds in the area of illegal gambling may be as high as $5 billion.[6]

More is involved than the traditional activities of organized crime.[7] White-collar crime may have an economic impact in our society as high as $100 billion, as high as or higher than the drug traffic itself.[8]

These figures must also be placed in context. The drug traffic at $79 billion, for example, is more than three and one-half times what we spend on tobacco ($20.7 billion) and a little less than twice what we spend for alcoholic beverages ($43.7 billion). It is, in fact, fast approaching what we spend for motor vehicles and parts ($89.7 billion) or furniture and household equipment ($86.3 billion).[9] No sane society can long permit such large sums to be acquired by criminal means and still hope to maintain its basic integrity.

The experience with the 1970 acts, however, has not been happy. Comparatively few assets have been forfeited under either the RICO or CCE statutes. In fact, federal investigative and prosecutive agencies only recently have begun to place an emphasis on asset forfeiture under the 1970 acts. More troubling, a series of court decisions has given the statutes an unnecessarily narrow reading on issues ranging from their scope to their implementation.[10] It is appropriate, therefore, to look at the historical background, enactment, and implementation of the RICO and CCE, as well as current proposals for reform.

Historical Background

That property should be forfeited by the owner under certain circumstances is a concept with ancient roots. Biblical,[11] Greek,[12] and Roman[13] law knew forms of forfeiture. So, too, did English law.

The forfeiture of property is one of the earliest sanctions of Anglo-Saxon law. Three types of forfeitures came to be distinguished: statutory forfeiture, forfeiture consequent to a criminal conviction and attainder, and deodand.

Statutes in England imposed a variety of forfeitures, principally as a means of tax enforcement. In the mid-seventeenth century, Parliament enacted the Navigation Acts, the broadest of the English forfeiture statutes, which required that shipping had to be in English-built, -owned, and -manned vessels, and provided that violations would result in the forfeiture of the ship and the goods it carried.[14] Suits for these forfeitures were commenced by civil information. They could be brought against a person *(in personam)* or against the thing to be forfeited *(in rem)*. Typically they were brought *in rem* against the vessel and the goods, as the owner could not be located or was beyond the jurisdiction of the court.[15]

Forfeiture consequent to a criminal conviction and attainder was, however, the oldest and best known. It was imposed on traitors and felons, who forfeited all of their personal and real property, not as a result of their conviction but their attainder, a pronouncement of legal death.[16] Attainder also means corruption of blood; that is, no descendant could ever trace a line of inheritance through the attainted ancestor. Forfeiture of lands related back to the time of the commission of the offense, voiding subsequent sales or incumbrances. Forfeiture of goods did not relate back, but transfers collusively made, that is, not *bona fide*, were not good against the Crown.

Deodands are sometimes spoken of as predecessors of the forfeiture statutes, but the historical evidence indicates that they were atypical.[17] An instrument of death replaced the slayer's kin as the object of vengeance. At first the instrument was taken and sold and the proceeds used to buy Masses for the victim.[18] Throughout the later Middle Ages, the king received the money, which provided a small, but steady source of revenue.

In the American colonies, the extent to which English law and practice should be adopted was a matter of great dispute.[19] Forfeitures did not follow any uniform practice. For example, forfeiture consequent to conviction and attainder was largely abolished in Massachusetts,[20] allowed to fall into disuse in New York,[21] but was fairly widely employed in Pennsylvania[22] and Virginia.[23] The acceptance of deodand presents a cloudier picture, and firm judgments cannot be made on the scope of its adoption.[24] Finally, while the Crown did not insist on most forfeitures, since the proceeds would have gone to the colonial governments, it did insist on the enforcement of the Navigation Acts, which by their terms were applicable to the colonies.[25] They were enforced in the vice-admiralty courts, not generally *in rem*, but *in personam*, and they were tried by the court without a jury.[26]

Following the Revolution, forfeiture consequent to conviction and attainder fell into disrepute. The Constitution itself forbade bills of attainder—legislative, not judicial, determinations of guilt.[27] It also limited corruption of blood and forfeitures of estate for treason to life estates.[28] In 1790, Congress abolished by statute both corruption of blood and forfeiture of estate as a consequence of federal criminal prosecutions.[29]

A variety of statutes, however, continued the practice of declaring specific forfeitures, which could be imposed in criminal or civil proceedings, either *in personam* or *in rem*. How a particular forfeiture was to be treated was a question of legislative intent.[30] So, too, was the time when the forfeiture was to take place, that is, at the time of the offense or at the time of the conviction.[31] The usual forfeiture in the federal courts, however, was patterned after the Navigation Acts, and it was imposed in an *in rem* proceeding. It was also early held that property could be forfeited without a prior criminal conviction[32] and that the time of forfeiture would relate back to the time of the offense, even as against a *bona fide* purchaser for value.[33] *In rem* forfeitures were rationalized by the personification fiction. Personal guilt was not implicated. The prosecution was brought not against the owner but the thing itself, and judgment was rendered against the whole world.

The Civil War brought about a radical change in the law of forfeiture. It quickly became evident that traditional treason prosecutions could not be brought against most rebels, for they were safely behind Confederate lines. Their life, liberty, and property—even where their property was not in the South—were beyond the power of northern courts, as *in absentia* prosecutions were not constitutionally possible. the solution hit on by the radicals in Congress was civil *in rem* forfeiture proceedings.[34] President Lincoln threatened a veto,[35] but when Congress responded by passing an explanatory joint resolution,[36] he signed the measures, which were eventually upheld by the Supreme Court.[37] Criminal *in personam* forfeiture proceedings then largely disappeared from the federal scene. Constitutional attacks on civil *in rem* forfeitures were also launched again when they were used during prohibition to suppress the traffic in illicit alcohol, but the Supreme Court turned them back on the basis of the precedents established in the post–Civil War era.[38] The constitutional validity of *in rem* civil forfeitures today now seems to be settled beyond serious question.[39]

The 1970 Acts: RICO and CCE

Scope

In RICO, Congress authorized two distinct forfeitures.[40] First, it authorized the forfeiture of any interest acquired through a violation of RICO. Second, it authorized the forfeiture of any interest affording a source of influence over any enterprise operated through a violation of RICO. Each is a criminal forfeiture. They can be imposed only after the return of a grand jury indictment specifying the interest to be forfeited,[41] a specific finding by a trial jury after a full criminal trial,[42] and the entry of a judgment by the court.[43]

Controversy has arisen over the scope of the forfeiture of interests acquired. The courts at first split on whether it extended to the proceeds of illicit transactions.[44] The Supreme Court resolved the split in *United States v. Russello*.[45]

The scope of the forfeiture of interests in enterprises has been read broadly. They have been held to extend to union offices,[46] corporate ownership,[47] and partnership interests.[48]

In CCE, Congress also authorized two distinct forfeitures.[49] First, it authorized the forfeiture of profit obtained by the operation of a drug enterprise. Second, it authorized the forfeiture of any interest affording a source of influence over any drug enterprise.

The CCE forfeitures are, of course, but a particularized effort to adapt the more generalized RICO forfeitures to the drug traffic. Little controversy has developed over their scope.[50] They too are criminal.

Protective Orders

In an effort to guarantee that assets subject to forfeiture will be available for execution after judgment, RICO and CCE authorize the pretrial issuance of restraining orders following the return of indictments specifying forfeitures.[51] The similarity between these orders and provisions for bail is manifest.[52] Nevertheless, the courts have encumbered them with procedural limitations not applicable to bail. To secure a restraining order, the government must show the likelihood of a conviction, the forfeiture of the property, and that the property might be dissipated before verdict.[53] Unlike in the comparable bail hearing,[54] asset hearings must conform to the rules of evidence.[55]

Time of Forfeiture

Neither RICO nor CCE specifies the time of forfeiture, that is, whether at the time of the commission of the offense or at some later date.[56] If the forfeiture takes place at the time of judgment but relates back to the time of the offense, questions are raised about the validity of various kinds of intermediate transfers.

Questions also are raised about the right of the government to trace and forfeit the proceeds realized from transfers for value or to seek the forfeiture of substitute assets in an amount equal to the value of the transferred assets.[57] The rights of innocent parties, either victims or good faith purchasers of the assets subject to forfeiture, must also be considered. With mixed results to date, the government has argued for the doctrine of relation back or at least the ability to void sham transactions.[58] Only RICO explicitly protects the rights of innocent parties.[59]

Conclusion

The enactment of RICO and CCE resulted from a national concern with the general impact of organized criminal activity on the nation and particularly with its effect on the national economy. In 1951, the Senate Special Committee to Investigate Organized Crime in Interstate Commerce, headed by Senator Estes Kefauver, began the first nationwide investigation into organized crime.[60] The committee's examination of organized crime's involvement in casino and other forms of illegal gambling and drugs and its infiltration into legitimate businesses raised the public's awareness of the seriousness of organized crime and its generation of illicit funds. The American Bar Association, in response to a request by Senator Kefauver, established the American Bar Association Commission on Organized Crime.[61] The commission examined various proposals to strengthen the law as it dealt with organized crime, including measures that recognized that "money [was] the key to power in the Underworld."[62] Those proposals, too, were reviewed by the President's Commission on Law Enforcement and Administration of Justice, which examined the effects of organized crime and other forms of crime on the national economy. After assessing its impact,[63] the commission concluded:

> Law enforcement's way of fighting organized crime has been primitive compared to organized crime's way of operating. Law enforcement must use methods at least as efficient as organized crime's. The public and law enforcement must make a full-scale commitment to destroy the power of organized crime groups.[64]

RICO and CCE were efforts by the Congress to respond to the findings of the crime commission.

Comparatively few assets have been forfeited under either RICO or CCE.[65] A variety of reasons account for that failure.[66] Until recently investigative and prosecutive agencies have not placed sufficient emphasis on forfeiture. Investigative and prosecutive expertise has been lacking. More troubling, not only has it been difficult to uncover the unlawful activities themselves,[67] it has also been difficult to find the assets or connect them with unlawful activity. Too often, they have been held in third-party hands or dissipated at the beginning of investigations.

Current efforts are being made to give asset forfeiture greater emphasis.[68] Greater attention, too, is being devoted to developing expertise. Finally, reform legislation is pending in Congress that would clarify the divisions that have developed in the courts over the scope of RICO and CCE and their implementation.[69] Accordingly the prospects for greater efforts at curtailing the flow of illicit funds in society are bright. It is premature, however, to predict how successful those efforts will prove to be.[70]

Notes

1. Organized Crime Control Act, Pub. L. No. 91-452, 84 Stat. 922 (1970), *codified at*, 18 U.S.C. § 1961 *et seq. See generally* Blakey, "The RICO Civil Fraud Action in Context: Reflections on *Bennett v. Berg*," 58 *Notre Dame Law* 237 (1982) (hereinafter cited as *RICO Civil Fraud)*; Blakey and Gettings, "Racketeer Influenced and Corrupt Organizations (RICO): Basic Concepts—Criminal and Civil Remedies," 53 *Temple* 1009 (1980). The defense counsel's perspective is reflected in Tarlow, "RICO: The New Darling of the Prosecutor's Nursery," 49 *Fordham L. Rev.* 165 (1980); Tarlow, "RICO Revisited," 17 *Ga. L. Rev.* 291 (1983).

2. Comprehensive Drug Abuse Prevention and Control Act, Pub. L. No. 91-513, 84 Stat. 1236 (1970), *codified at*, 21 U.S.C. § 801 *et seq.*

3. For an excellent review of the historical materials, *see generally*, Note, "Bane of American Forfeiture Law," 62 *Cornell L. Rev.* 708 (1977).

4. N.Y. Times, Oct. 15, 1982, at 11, col. 6. Those funds also quickly find their way into the legitimate market. *See Forfeiture of Narcotics Proceeds: Hearings before the Subcomm. on Criminal Justice of the Senate Judiciary Comm.*, 96th Cong., 2d Sess. at 20 (1975) (testimony of William J. Anderson, Director, General Government Division, General Accounting Office) (estimate of $1 billion invested in Florida real estate from 1977 to 1978). Most concede that the flow of illicit funds in the area of drug is high. Rightly, not all accept at face value the current estimates. Reuter, "The (continued) Vitality of Mythical Numbers," 75 *Pub. Int.* 135 (1984). For a comprehensive analysis of the mechanics of the flow of funds, *see* Staff Study, *Crime and Secrecy: The Use of Offshore Banks and Companies*, S. Rep. No. 21, 98th Cong., 1st Sess. (Comm. Print 1983).

5. The 1972 estimate was $20 billion. Blakcy and Goldsmith, "Criminal Redistribution of Stolen Property: The Need for Law Reform," 74 *Mich. L. Rev.* 1511, 1517 (1976). In the light of inflation, the higher figure is appropriate today. In 1980, for example, the National Crime Survey reported $9.5 billion in losses from only personal robberies, personal and house larcenies, household burglaries, and privately owned motor vehicle theft. U.S. Department of Justice, *Report to the Nation on Crime and Justice: The Data*, at 22 (1983).

6. The flow of illicit funds in the area of gambling is a matter of dispute. *Compare* Final Report of the Commission on the Review of National Policy toward Gambling, *Gambling in America* at 63–65 (1976) (hereinafter *Gambling)*, *with* Kallick and Kaufman, "Micro and Macro

Dimensions of Gambling in the United States," 35 *J. of Soc. Issues* 19 (1979). The $5 billion figure represents the estimates of the social scientists who conducted a national survey for the commission. The Department of Justice, however, told the commission that its estimate was between $29 billion and $39 billion. *Gambling* at 63. The Commission expressed reservations about the lower figure. *Id.* at 63–65. Other estimates of the handle and take, too, are higher. Report of the Task Force on Legalized Gambling, *Easy Money* (Fund for the City of New York and the Twentieth Century Fund, New York) (1974) (handle $22.9 billion, gross take $3.5 billion, net take $1.6 billion). Whichever estimates are used, gambling cannot be accepted any longer as the chief source of income for organized crime, as it was in 1967. President's Commission on Law Enforcement and Administration of Justice, *The Challenge of Crime in a Free Society* at 188 (1967) (hereinafter *Challenge*). For other estimates of the flow of illicit funds, see Department of the Treasury, Internal Revenue Service, *Income Tax Compliance Research: Estimates for 1973–81* at 35–39 (July 1983) (unreported income for 1981: drugs ($23.4 billion), gambling ($3.4 billion), prostitution ($7.4 billion)). The service has recently completed more comprehensive estimates, but they are not yet public. On the difficulties of estimating the size of various aspects of the underground economy, see *Growth by the Underground Economy, 1950–81: Some Evidence from the Current Population Survey.* S. Rep. No. 122, 98th Cong., 1st Sess. 2–4 (1983).

7. *Organized Crime* is a phrase with many meanings. It is much like the fictional crime portrayed in Akira Kursawa's 1950 film, *Rashoman,* in which a ninth-century nobleman's bride is raped by a bandit, and the nobleman lies dead. The film portrays versions of the double crime from the perspectives of each of the three participants and a witness. Each version is different. So it is with the definition of organized crime. Some have seen nothing and decided that nothing was there. *See, e.g.,* Hawkins, "God and the Mafia," 14 *Pub. Int. 24* (1969). Others, examining the phenomenon from an anthropological perspective, have seen a "social system." *See, e.g.,* F. Ianni, *A Family Business* (1972). One commentator, relying on press accounts, has seen only a public relations gimmick. D. Smith, *The Mafia Mystique* (1975). The organizational theorist sees a functional division of labor. D. Cressey, *Theft of the Nation* (1969). Some lawyers have seen it as a conspiracy. Blakey, "Aspects of the Evidence Gathering Process in Organized Crime Cases: A Preliminary Analysis," *Task Force Reform: Organized Crime: The President's Commission on Law Enforcement and Administration of Justice* at 80, 81–93 (1967). The President's Crime Commission in 1967 adopted a view that termed conspiratorial behavior "organized crime" when its organizational sophistication reached a level where division of labor included positions for an "enforcer" of violence and a "corrupter" of the legitimate processes of our society. *Id.* at 8. The particular organized crime syndicate known as the Mafia was termed only the "core" of organized crime; it was not identified with it. *Id.* at 6. The tendency of some to identify organized crime with the Mafia has been decried by no less than the sponsor of the Organized Crime Control Act, Senator John L. McClellan. *Gambling* at 181–182 ("in none of the hearings or in the processing of legislation in which I have been involved has the term been used

in this circumscribed fashion"). That other ethnic groups are deeply involved in organized crime on both the syndicate and enterprise level seems evident. *Pennsylvania Crime Commission, 1980 Report: A Decade of Organized Crime* at 18–20 ("Black Mafia" in Philadelphia). For a further breakdown of the concept into "syndicate," "enterprise," and "venture," *see Electronic Surveillance: Report of the National Commission for the Review of Federal and State Laws Relating to Wiretapping and Electronic Surveillance* at 190–192 (1976) (concurring statement of Commissioner Blakey). Ultimately, too, the definition of organized crime is a question not only of perspective but of purpose. Different professions may legitimately define it differently for different purposes. Even the same profession may legitimately define it differently in different contexts. Accordingly, no one ought to expect a single definition to command universal adherence. G. Blakey, R. Goldstock, and C. Rogovin, *Racket Bureaus: Investigation and Prosecution of Organized Crime, National Institute of Law Enforcement and Criminal Justice* at 3 (1978). Only those who believe that people serve words rather than that words serve people think otherwise. See C. Dodgson ("Lewis Carroll"), *Through the Looking Glass and What Alice Found There* at 106 (Signet Classical 1960) ("When I use a word," Humpty Dumpty said, "it means just what I choose it to mean—neither more nor less.")

8. The most comprehensive study of white-collar crime, particularly fraud, done in recent years was published under the auspices of the Chamber of Commerce of the United States in 1974. Including bankruptcy fraud, bribes, kickbacks and payoffs, consumer fraud, embezzlement, insurance fraud, receiving stolen property, and securities fraud, the estimate was $40 billion. Chamber of Commerce of the United States, *White Collar Crime: Everyone's Problem, Everyone's Loss* at 6 (1974) (hereinafter *Chamber*). The *Chamber* figure was accepted and icnreased for inflation to 44 in 1976 by the Joint Economic Committee of the Contress. *White Collar Crime: The Problem and the Federal Response,* Subcomm. on Crime of the Comm. on the Judiciary, 95th Cong., 2nd Sess. at 10 (1978). More recently, the figure has been put at between $44 billion and $100 billion. *Hearings on the Department of State, Justice, Commerce, the Judiciary and Related Agencies' Appropriations in 1981: House Subcomm. of the Comm. of Appropriations,* 96th Cong., 2nd Sess. 17 (1980) (testimony of William H. Webster, director of the Federal Bureau of Investigation). The 1974 figures, too, may have understated the scope of the problem. Insurance fraud, for example, was put at $2 billion. *Chamber* at 6. The American Insurance Association today, however, estimates that 15 to 20 percent of all claims are fraudulent— up 5 to 6 percent in just ten years. *N.Y. Times* July 6, 1980, at 27, col. 1. Currently fraudulent claims may exceed $11 billion each year, and since the typical insurance company must generate $1.25 in premiums for every $1 it pays in claims, policy holders are paying an extra $13.75 billion in premiums. *Id.* at 28, col. 4.

9. U.S. Dept. of Comm., Bureau of the Census, *Statistical Abstract of the United States: 1982–1983* at 422.

10. This trend in the decisions cannot be reconciled with the text of the statute. RICO contains a "liberal construction" directive. 94 Stat. 947. The Supreme court recognized its virtually unique status in federal criminal

law in *Russello v. United States*, 104 S. Ct. 296, 302 (1983). It is not unique in state law. It had its origins in the codification movement of the nineteenth century. Edward Livingston suggested the rejection of the old common law rule of strict construction in the far-sighted code he drafted for Louisiana between 1820 and 1825. I E. Livingston, *Complete Works on Criminal Jurisprudence* at 231 (1873 ed.) and II, *id.* at 14 ("All penal laws whatever are to be construed according to the plain import of their words"). Livingston's suggestion for Louisiana was followed by David Dudley Field in his influential draft of codes of penal law and criminal procedure for New York. *Penal Code of the State of New York* at 5 (1865 ed.) ("fair import"); *The Code of Criminal Procedure* at 470–471 (1850 ed.) ("liberally construed"). He noted that the old rule had no support in any "principle of substantial justice, and . . . [its] highest aim, practically considered, seem[ed] to be, to render the law inconsistent with its spirit, and as a consequence, absurd and ridiculous." *Id.* Indeed judicial hostility to change through legislation was so common at that time "that it became standard practice in drafting statutes to insert a preamble declaring that the statute should be liberally construed." D. Wigdor, *Roscoe Pound: Philosopher of Law* at 174 (1974). In fact, a majority of states today has abolished the common law rule either by expressly abrogating it or adopting some variation of "fair import" or "liberal construction." The statutes are collected in *RICO Civil Fraud* at 245 n. 25. On the relation between the liberal construction clause and the rule of lenity, *see id.* at 288–290, n. 150.

    11. *Exodus* 21:28. ("If an ox gore a man or woman, that they die: then the ox shall be surely stoned, and his flesh shall not be eaten; but the owner of the ox shall be quit.")

    12. See O. Holmes, *The Common Law* at 8 (1881).

    13. 7 *Twelve Tables* 1, *translated in,* I Scott, *The Civil Law* at 69 (1932). ("If a quadraped causes injury to anyone, let the owner tend him the estimated amount of the damage; and if he is unwilling to accept it, the owner shall . . . surrender the animal that caused the injury.")

    14. L. Harper, *The English Navigation Laws: A Seventeenth-Century Experiment in Social Engineering* at 109, 387–414 (1964).

    15. *See,* III W. Blackstone, *Commentaries* at 262.

    16. IV W. Blackstone, *Commentaries* at 374–381. "Felony" under early English law included any breach of the feudal engagement. M. Radin, *Anglo-American Legal History* at 234 (1936). As such, it resulted in the forfeiture of the feudal estate to the lord. *Id.* at 240. Chattels went to the king, whose regalian rights included all ownerless property—*bona vacantia,* which is what an outlaw's property was. *Id.*

    17. *Compare Calero-Toledo v. Pearson Yacht Leasing Co.,* 416 U.S. 663, 680–683 (1974) *with* Note, *supra,* n. 3 at 771–772.

    18. *Calero-Toledo v. Pearson Yacht Leasing Co.,* 416 U.S. 663, 681 (1974).

    19. I J. Story, *Commentaries on the Constitution of the United States* at §§ 163–165, 187–197 (Cooley 4th ed. 1873).

    20. V N. Dane, *A General Abridgement and Digest of American Law* at 4 (1824).

    21. J. Goebel and T. Naughten, *Law Enforcement in Colonial New York*

at 712–713, 716 (1944). New York juries simply found nothing to forfeit. *Id.*

22. *See, e.g., Respublica v. Doan*, 1 U.S. (1 Dall.) 90, 95 (Pa. 1784) (forfeiture following outlawry).

23. A. Scott, *Criminal Law in Colonial Virginia* at 109 (1930).

24. *Compare*, J. Goebel and T. Naughton, *supra*, n. 21 at 717 *with* S. Pennypacker, *Pennsyvlania Colonial Cases* at 70 (1892).

25. *See, e.g.*, 12 Car. 2, C. 18 ch II (1660).

26. *See generally* Wroth, "The Massachusetts Vice Admiralty Court and the Federal Admiralty Jurisdiction," 6 *Am. J. Legal Hist.* 250 (1962).

27. *U.S. Const.* art I, § 9, cl. 3.

28. *U.S. Const.* art III, § 3, cl. 2.

29. 1 Stat. 117, c. 9, § 24 (1790), *codified at* 18 U.S.C. § 3563. *See United States v. Grande*, 620 F.2d 1026, 1039 (4th Cir.) ("Nothing . . . suggests that either article III or the 1790 statute was intended to prohibit anything other than corruption of blood or forfeiture of estate as imposed at common law."), *cert denied sub nom. Berg v. United States*, 449 U.S. 919 (1980).

30. *United States v. 1960 Bags of Coffee*, 12 U.S. (8 Cranch) 398 (1814).

31. *Id.* The Supreme Court described as "settled doctrine" in *United States v. Stowell*, 133 U.S. 1, 16–17 (1890) the rule that forfeiture takes place "immediately upon the commission" of the offense and the right to the property then vests in the government, although it was not "perfected" until a judicial decree was issued.

32. *The Palmyra*, 25 U.S. (12 Wheat)1 (1827) at 15. Nevertheless, the Court held in *Coffey v. United States*, 116 U.S. 436, 444–445 (1886) that if there were an acquitter in a criminal proceeding, there could not be a subsequent *in rem* forfeiture in a civil proceeding. *Coffey* was disapproved of in *United States v. One Assortment of 89 Firearms*, 34 Crim. L. Reprtr. 3053 (2-22-84) (neither double jeopardy nor collateral estoppel precludes civil *in rem* forfeiture after criminal acquittal; civil character of proceeding question of legislative intent).

33. *See supra*, nn. 30 and 31.

34. *See generally* J. Randall, *The Confiscation of Property During the Civil War* (1913).

35. Lincoln had two objections: confiscation was not limited to a life estate, and the proceeding was *in rem. Cong. Globe*, 37th Cong., 2d Sess. 3406 (1862).

36. The joint resolution responded by limiting them to a life estate. *Id.* at App. 423. It did not meet Lincoln's second objection.

37. *See* III C. Warren, *The Supreme Court in United States History* at 138–139 (1922).

38. *J.W. Goldsmith, Jr.-Grant Co. v. United States*, 254 U.S. 505 (1921).

39. *Calero-Toledo v. Pearson Yacht Leasing Co.*, 416 U.S. 663, 680–683 (1974).

40. 18 U.S.C. § 1963(a) provides: "Whoever violates any provision of section 1962 of this chapter shall be fined not more than $25,000 or imprisoned not more than twenty years, or both, and shall forfeit to the United States (1) any interest he has acquired or maintained in violation of section

1962, and (2) any interest in, security of, claim against, or property or contractual right of any kind affording a source of influence over, any enterprise which he has established, operated, controlled, conducted, or participated in the conduct of, in violation of section 1962."

41. Fed. R. Crim. P. 7 (c)(2).

42. Fed. R. Crim. P. 31 (e).

43. Fed. R. Crim. P. 32 (b)(2). The forfeiture is mandatory. *United States v. Hess*, 691 F.2d 188, 190 (4th Cir. 1982); *United States v. L'Hoste*, 609 F.2d 796, 809–13 (5th Cir.), *reh'g denied*, 615 F.2d 383, (5th Cir.), *cert. denied*, 449 U.S. 833 (1980). *But see, United States v. Huber*, 603 F.2d 387, 397 (2d Cir. 1979) (discretion in application), *cert. denied*, 445 U.S. 927 (1980). Provision is made, however, for mitigation or remission. 18 U.S.C. § 1963 (c) (discretion of attorney general). The mandatory forfeiture is an essential feature of the effort to make the threat to take the profit out of crime swift, sure and severe, a feature necessary if the fruits of crime are to lose their beguiling lure. R. Posner, *Economic Analysis of Law* § 7.2 (2d ed 1977). Making the forfeitures *in personam* and criminal rather than *in rem* and civil met Lincoln's second objection. *See supra*, n. 35.

44. *Compare United States v. Marubeni America Corp.*, 611 F.2d 763, 765–770 (9th Cr. 1980) (limited to interest in enterprise) *and United States v. McManigal*, 708 F.2d 276, 283–287 (7th Cir. 1983) (same), *with United States v. Martino*, 648 F.2d 367, 407–409 (5th Cir. 1981) (same), *rev'd en banc*, 681 F.2d 952, 954–961 (5th Cir.) (extends to proceeds), *affirmed, Russello v. United States*, 104 S. Ct. 296 (1983). For a powerful critique of *Marubeni, see* Tojanowski, "RICO Forfeitures: Tracing and Procedures Appendix," in I *Materials on RICO* (Cornell Institute on Organized Crime, G. Blakey editor 1980). Among other things, *Marubeni* cannot be reconciled with RICO's liberal construction clause, 84 Stat. 947. *See, RICO Civil Fraud* at 245 n. 25 and 288 n. 150 (analysis of liberal construction). Acquired interests in an enterprise have also been held to include commercial real estate. *United States v. Godoy*, 678 F.2d 84, 86 (9th Cir. 1982) (interest in enterprise acquired under § 1963 (a)(1) forfeited), *cert. denied*, 104 S. Ct. 390 (1983).

45. 104 S. Ct. 296 (1983); *see supra*, n. 44. In *Russello*, the prosecution sought to forfeit the proceeds secured through an arson fraud scheme. In upholding the forfeiture, the Court observed: "The legislative history clearly demonstrates that the RICO statute was intended to provide new weapons of unprecedented scope for an assault upon organized crime and its economic roots. . . . Congress emphasized the need to fashion new remedies in order to achieve its far-reaching objectives. . . . The legislative history leaves no doubt that, in the view of Congress, the economic power of organized crime derived from its huge illegal profits. . . . Congress could not have hoped successfully to attack organized crime's economic roots without reaching racketeering profits. . . . It is true that Congress viewed the RICO statute in large part as a response to organized crime's infiltration of legitimate enterprises. . . . But Congress' concerns were not limited to infiltration.

The broader goal was to remove the profit from organized crime by separating the racketeer from his dishonest gains" (104 S. Ct. at 302–303).

46. *United States v. Rubin,* 559 F.2d 975, 990–993 (5th Cir. 1977), *vacated and remanded,* 439 U.S. 810 (1978), *reinstated in relevant part,* 591 F.2d 278 (5th Cir.), *cert. denied,* 444 U.S. 864 (1979).

47. *United States v. Huber,* 603 F.2d 387, 397 (2d Cir. 1979), *cert. denied,* 445 U.S. 927 (1980).

48. *United States v. Walsh,* 700 F.2d 846, 857 (2d Cir. 1983). Nineteen states currently have some form of RICO Statute: Ariz. Rev. Stat. Ann. § 13-2312 (1978); Cal. Penal Code § 186 (West Supp. 1983); Colo. Rev. Stat. § 18-17-101 (1981); Conn. Gen. Stat. Ann. § 53-393 (West Supp. 1983-1984); Fla. Stat. Ann. § 895.01 (West Supp. 1983); Ga. Code Ann. § 16-14-1 (1982); Hawaii Rev. Stat. § 842-1 (1976); Idaho Code § 18-7801 (Supp. 1983); Ill. Ann. Stat. ch. 56-1/2, § 1651 (Smith-Hurd Supp. 1983); Ind. Code Ann. § 35-45-6-1 (Burns Supp. 1982); Nev. Rev. Stat. § 207.4-17 (1983); N.J. Stat. Ann. § 2C:41 (West 1982); N.M. Stat. Ann. § 30-42-1 (B.B. 1982); N.D. Cent. Code § 12.1-06.1 (Supp. 1983); Or. Rev. Stat. § 166-715 (1981); 18 Pa. Cons. Stat. § 911 (1978); R.I. Gen. Laws § 7-15-1 (Supp. 1982); Utah Code Ann. § 76-10-1601 (Supp. 1983); Wis. Stat. Ann. § 946.80 (West Supp. 1983). Ten of these statutes include some form of civil *in rem* forfeiture, which was modeled not on RICO but the CCE civil provisions. *See infra* n. 49. Such forfeiture provisions are found in Ariz. Rev. Stat. Ann. § 13-2314 (Supp. 1983); Colo. Rev. Stat. § 18-17-106 (Supp. 1983); Fla. Stat. Ann. § 895.05 (West Supp. 1983); Ga. Code Ann. § 16-14-7 (1982); Ind. Code Ann. § 34-4-30.5-4 (Burns Supp. 1982); Nev. Rev. Stat. § 207.4-17 (1983); N.J. Stat. Ann. § 2C:41-4 (West 1982); N.D. Cent. Code § 12.1-06.1-05 (Supp. 1983); Or. Rev. Stat. § 166.725 (3) procedural (1) and (2)—types of property (1981); Wis. Stat. Ann. § 946.86 (West Supp. 1983). Six of these statutes facially allow seizure without process under certain guidelines: Colo. Rev. Stat. § 18-17-106 (Supp. 1983); Fla. Stat. Ann. § 895.05 (West Supp. 1983); Ga. Code Ann. § 16-14-7 (1982); Ind. Code Ann. § 34-4-30.5-4 (Burns Supp. 1982); Nev. Rev. Stat. § 207.4-17 (1983); Or. Rev. Stat. § 166.725 (3) (1981). The federal courts disagree on the need for process under the federal drug act. *See, e.g., United States v. One 1978 Mercedes Benz, Four-Door Sedan,* 711 F.2d 1297, 1300-03 (5th Cir. 1983) (§ 881 civil forfeiture upheld) (conflicting cases on need for process reviewed). The facial constitutionality of seizure without prior warrant under the broad language of the civil *in rem* RICO statutes is before the Supreme Court in *Cole v. Georgia,* No. 83-322, *cert. granted,* 34 Crim. L. Reptr. 4073 (11-7-83). A decision is expected before the end of the term.

49. 21 U.S.C. § 848(a)(2) provides: "Any person who is convicted under paragraph (1) of engaging in a continual criminal enterprise shall forfeit to the United States—(A) the profits obtained by him in such enterprise, and (B) any of his interest in, claim against, or property or contractual rights of any kind affording a source of influence over, such enterprise."

The statute also contained an *in rem* civil forfeiture. 21 U.S.C. 881(b)(4).

The language of the federal statute was incorporated in section 505 of the Uniform Controlled Substances Act 9 U.L.A. 612-13 (1979). That uniform statute has been substantially adopted by forty-six states, plus the District of Columbia, Puerto Rico, and the Virgin Islands. *Id.* at 78 (Cum. Supp. 1983).

50. *See, e.g., United States v. Murillo,* 709 F.2d 1298, 1299 (9th Cir. 1983) (§ 848 criminal forfeiture upheld).

51. 18 U.S.C. § 1963(b) provides: "In any action brought by the United States under this section, the district courts of the United States shall have jurisdiction to enter such restraining orders or prohibitions, or to take such other actions, including, but not limited to, the acceptance of satisfactory performance bonds, in connection with any property or other interests subject to forfeiture under this section, as it shall deem proper."

21 U.S.C. § 848(d) provides: "The district courts of the United States (including courts in the territories or possessions of the United States having jurisdiction under subsection (a) of this section) shall have jurisdiction to enter such restraining orders or prohibitions, or to take such other actions, including the acceptance of satisfactory performance bonds, in connection with any property or otherinterest subject to forfeiture under this section, as they shall deem proper."

52. *See, e.g., United States v. Scalzitti,* 08 F. Supp. 1014, 1015 (W.D. Pa. 1975), *appeal dismissed,* 556 F.2d 569 (3d Cir. 1977).

For a highly critical review of these procedures, *see* Reed and Gill, "RICO Forfeitures, Forfeitable "Interests," and Procedural Due Process," 62 *N.C. Rev.* 57 (1983). For a more restrained analysis, see Note, "Due Process in Preliminary Proceedings Under RICO and CCE," 83 *Colum. L. Rev.* 2068 (1983).

53. *See, e.g., United States v. Spilotro,* 680 F.2d 612, 616, 618, 619 n. 4 (9th Cir. 1982). Apparently the court was concerned with the due process implications of *Fuentes v. Shevin,* 407 U.S. 67 (1972). *Fuentes,* however, is not apposite generally to forfeitures, *Calero-Toledo v. Pearson Yacht Leasing Co.,* 416 U.S. 663, 680–683 (1974), as it is also not applicable to the initiation of the criminal process itself. *Gerstein v. Pugh,* 420 U.S. 103, 122–125 (1975) ("The relatively simple civil procedures . . . are inapposite and irrelevant in the wholly different context of the criminal justice system.") *Spilotro* was wrongly decided. If the provisions for bail carry lesser protections than the provisions for asset restraining orders, property will recieve greater protection than liberty, a result hard to square with our fundamental legal attitudes.

54. 18 U.S.C. § 3146(f) ("need not conform"); *United States v. Graewe,* 689 F.2d 54, 56–58 (6th Cir. 1982) (use of hearsay to deny bail based on danger to witnesses).

55. *See, e.g., United States v. Veon,* 538 F. Supp. 237, 248–249 (E.D. Cal. 1982). *Contra United States v. Harvey,* 560 F. Supp. 1040, 1085–1088 (S.D. Fla. 1983) (hearsay proper).

56. Congress knew full well it was drawing on the "ancient doctrine of criminal forfeiture." S. Rep. No. 91-617, 91st Cong., 1st Sess. 78–80 (1969). It is difficult to see how the common law rule of relation back would not be applicable. *See supra,* n. 31, and *infra* n. 58. The rejection of the

concept of relation back in *United States v. McManigal*, 708 F.2d 276, 287–290 (7th Cir. 1983) is contrary to congressional intent.

57. *See, e.g., United States v. Veon*, 549 F. Supp. 274, 282–284 (E.D. Cal. 1982) (prosecution has right to trace proceeds into and out of property into which they are invested). Tracing is provided for in the law of constructive trusts. *Restatement of Restitution* § 160. Reaching substitute assets is provided for in the law of equitable liens. *See also* V A. Scott, *Trusts* § 508 (where "a conscious wrongdoer uses the property of another in acquiring other property; the person whose property is so used is entitled at his option either to enforce a constructive trust or to enforce an equitable lien upon the property so acquired.") For two cases involving tracing, *see, United States v. Parness*, 503 F.2d 430, 436 (2d Cir. 1974), *cert. denied*, 429 U.S. 820 (1976) and *United States v. McNary*, 620 F.2d 621, 628 (7th Cir. 1980).

58. *Compare United States v. Long*, 654 F.2d 911, 916–917 (3d Cir. 1981) (transfer before indictment under CCE voided) *with United States v. McManigal*, 708 F.2d 276, 287–290 (7th Cir. 1983) (relation back theory rejected under RICO, but possibility of void transfer not to innocent purchaser noted). *See also United States v. Veon*, 549 F. Supp. 274, 280 n. 13 (E.D. Cal. 1982) (*lis pendens* notice struck under CCE since no interest in property until judgment). Unexamined in the cases to date is the impact of various fraudulent conveyance statutes. *See generally* Note, "Good Faith and Fraudulent Conveyances," 97 *Harv. L. Rev.* 495 (1983). At least since the time of Elizabeth I, such conveyances have been voidable, 13 Eliz. ch. 5 (1570). Generally a suit may be maintained to set aside a transfer of property made to avoid the payment of a fine or penalty. *Pierce v. United States*, 255 U.S. 398, 401–402 (1921) (Brandeis, J.) ("The corporation cannot disable itself from responding [to a prospective fine] by distributing its property among its stockholders and leaving remediless those having valid claims.") Unfortunately, prosecutors seem to be unaware of their rights under these laws.

59. 18 U.S.C. § 1963(c) ("due provision for the rights of innocent persons."). Victims of criminal conduct should be given priority in the distribution of the proceeds of any forfeiture sale. *See, e.g., United States v. One (1) 254 Ft. Freighter, the M/V Andoria*, 570 F. Supp. 413, 415 (E.D. La. 1983) (tort liens rank fourth).

60. *See generally* E. Kefauver, *Crime in America* (1951). The committee's origins lay in work done in California by then Governor Earl Warren, who created the California Crime Commission, which conducted a comprehensive review of organized crime in California. L. Katcher, *Earl Warren: A Political Biography* at 243–247 (1967). At the time, the work of the committee was not well received. *See* J. Wilson, "The Kefauver Committee 1950," 5 *Congress Investigates: A Documented History 1792–1974* at 3439 (A. Schlesinger, Jr., and R. Burns ed. 1975). Significantly, at the beginning of the probe, "Attorney General McGrath [said] that the Justice Department had no persuasive evidence that a 'national crime syndicate' . . . [existed]." *Id.* 3450. Kefauver made an effort to offer the evidence, but it did not persuade scholars. *See, e.g.,* W. Moore, *The Kefauver Committee and the Politics of Crime 1950–1952* at 241 (1974) ("debatable judgments on the structure

of organized crime"). Senator Kefauver's investigation into organized crime was continued by Senator John L. McClellan. A major focus of the McClellan committee's efforts was on the infamous Appalachian organized crime gathering in upstate New York in 1957 and the testimony of the Mafia informer, Joseph Valachi. That work, too, had its academic critics. A. Schlesinger, *A Thousand Days: John F. Kennedy in the White House* at 696 (1965) ("criminologists . . . skeptical of . . . a centrally organized . . . Mafia"); A. Schlesinger, *Robert Kennedy and His Times* at 303 (1978) (skeptic position "more persuasive"). Evidence obtained more recently by the Department of Justice and presented in court supports the Senate investigations of Kefauver and McClellan, not their critics. *Compare United States v. Bufalino*, 285 F.2d 408, 419 (2d Cir. 1960) (Clark J., concurring) ("not a shred of legal evidence that the Appalachian gathering was illegal") *with United States v. Bufalino*, 683 F.2d 639, 647 (2d Cir. 1982), *cert. denied*, 103 S. Ct. 727 (1983) (Bufalino, who was at Appalachian, was a member of "La Costra Nostra, an organization whose members performed murders for one another as a matter of professional courtesy"); *United States v. Brooklier*, 685 F.2d 1208, 1213 (9th Cir. 1982). (prosecution of "crime family" of Los Angeles) ("Appellants are members of La Cosa Nostra, a secret national organization engaged in a wide range of racketeering activities, including murder, extortion, gambling, and loansharking"); *United States v. Riccobene*, 709 F.2d 214, 217 (3d Cir. 1983) (prosecution of "crime family" of Philadelphia); and *United States v. Licavoli*, 725 F.2d 1040, 1043 (6th Cir. 1984) (prosecution of "crime family" of Cleveland).

61. *Organized Crime Control:* Hearing on S. 30 and Related Proposals Before Subcomm. No. 5 of the House Comm. on the Judiciary, 91 Cong., 2d Sess. at 544 (1979) (testimony of Edward L. Wright, the President-elect of the American Bar Association).

62. *Id.*

63. President's Comm'n. on Law Enforcement and Administration of Justice, *Task Force Report: Crime and Its Impact—An Assessment (1967).*

64. *Challenge* at 200.

65. In the period 1970 to 1980, for example, RICO and CCE indictments were returned in ninety-nine narcotics cases. Assets forfeited and potentially forfeited amounted to only $35 million. *See* Testimony of William J. Anderson, *supra*, n. 4 at 18. Indeed, of fifty successfully prosecuted cases, thirty-seven resulted in no criminal forfeitures. The experience is not better in general prosecutions against heads of major organized crime families. *Organized Crime in America:* hearings before the Comm. on the Judiciary of the United States Senate, 98th Cong. 1st Sess. at 78–79 (1983) (testimony of William H. Webster, Director, Federal Bureau of Investigation) (indictment of eleven leaders of families in Los Angeles, California, Pittston, Pennsylvania, Phoenix, Arizona, Kansas City, Missouri, Cleveland, Ohio, New Orleans, Louisiana, New York, New York, Philadelphia, Pennsylvania, and Denver, Colorado, involving four RICO charges, but not forfeitures). *See also Forfeiture of Narcotics Proceeds, supra* n. 4 at 142 (discussion of reasons why no forfeiture sought in *United States v. Barnes*, 604 F.2d 121 (2d Cir. 1979), *cert. denied*, 446 U.S. 907 (1980)).

66. *See, e.g., Forfeiture in Drug Cases: Hearings on H.R. 2648, H.R.*

2910, H.R. 4110, H.R. 5371: Before the Subcomm. on Crime of the House Comm. of the Judiciary, 96th Cong., 1st and 2nd Sess., 223–224 (1983) (testimony of Irvin B. Nathan, Deputy Attorney General): "Discovering a defendant's assets, securing them, providing their relationship to his crimes and seizing them after judgment are extremely difficult, time-consuming tasks which most federal investigations and prosecutors are not particularly well equipped to handle. Sophisticated criminals, with access to top-flight lawyers and accountants, can readily conceal their assets. The assets can be kept in the names of nominees, in secret bank accounts overseas, in shell corporations or run through money laundering operations. Even when assets are uncovered, and title is proven, there are evidentiary problems in attempting to link the assets to criminal activities. Finally, prosecutors are concerned that introducing detailed evidence relating to forfeitable assets may prolong and make more complex the criminal trial." *See also Stronger Federal Effort Needed in Fight against Organized Crime: Report by Comptroller General of the United States* at 31–34 (1981) (problems in criminal forfeiture: (1) uncertain status of assets, (2) third party holdings, and (3) dissipation prior to seizure); *Asset Forfeiture—A Seldom Used Tool in Combatting Drug Trafficking, Report of Comptroller General of the United States* at 30–42 (1981) (same). Little effort, too, is made to safeguard assets when they are seized. *Better Care and Disposal of Seized Cars, Boats and Planes Should Save Money and Benefit Law Enforcement: Report by The Comptroller General of the United States* (1983). Even when the assets are cash, they are often not deposited in interest-bearing accounts. *N.Y. Times,* Jan. 13, 1984, at 10, col. 4 (Grace Panel terms loss of $50 million each year "bureaucratic absurdity").

67. Little evidence exists that current law enforcement resource commitment and strategy are having a significant impact on drug traffic. *See generally Federal Drug Interdiction Efforts Need Strong Central Oversight: Report by the Comptroller General of the United States* (1983). Federal expenditures in drug control programs amount to $1 billion each year, yet only 2 to 5 percent of the heroin, for example, is diverted. *N.Y. Times,* Oct. 15, 1982, at 11, col. 6. Overall, less than 10 percent of all drug traffic entering the country is intercepted. *N.Y. Times,* Nov. 6, 1982, at 6, col. 1. For the most comprehensive study of the federal effort, *see* S. Rep. No. 1039, 94th Cong., 2d Sess. (1976). A number of changes have been made since 1976, but the traffic in drugs continues to grow.

Today the traffic in illicit drugs is in fact the major source of income for organized criminal groups. Illegal drugs "generated $64 billion in retail sales in 1979 compared to $50 billion in 1978 and 48 billion in 1977." *The National Intelligence Consumers Comm., The Supply of Drugs to the U.S. Illicit Market From Foreign and Domestic Sources in 1979,* at 5 (1979). The rise "was principally the result of increased consumption of cocaine, marihuana and dangerous drugs." *Id.* The 1980 figure is 79. *See, supra,* n. 4. Profit margins are incredibly high. *See generally* S. Rep. No. 887, 96th Cong., 2d Sess. (1980). The cocaine traffic is illustrative. A South American farmer sells 500 kilos of coca leaves for approximately $250, which ultimately produces one kilo of cocaine hydrochloride; it, in turn, is then cut to about 12 percent purity and sold at the street level for $800,000. *Id.* at 13. The traffic in most drugs is also highly organized. *Organized Crime and the Use of Violence: Hearings Before the Perm. Subcomm. on Investigations of the Senate Comm. on Governmental Affairs*, 96th Cong., 2d Sessl., 61–62 (1980) (testimony of Peter B. Bensinger, Director, (Administrator) Drug Enforcement Administration) ("sophisticated organized criminal syndicates with a corporate-like structure and motivated by power and profit").

68. *See* Testimony of William H. Webster, *supra*, n. 65 at 91 ("money is what it is all about").

69. *See, e.g.*, S. 1762, 98th Cong., 1st Sess. (1983), *as reported*, S. Rep. No. 98-225, 98th Cong., 1st Sess. (1983). The committee report includes a comprehensive analysis of the difficulties experienced in the enforcement of RICO and CCE forfeitures. *Id.* at 191–197 (scope too limited, preforfeiture transfers and legal impediments to efforts to prevent them, inefficiency of dual proceeding (crime prosecution followed by civil forfeiture proceeding), and high costs associated with the process without offsetting benefits for agencies of successful forfeitures). Title III, Comprehensive Forfeiture Act of 1983, would amend RICO and CCE. It explicitly includes proceeds within interests to be forfeited, provides for substitute forfeitures, makes provision for preindictment and postindictment restraining orders with the government's showings considerably lightened in the postindictment stage, and makes the rules of evidence inapplicable to hearings on restraining orders. Unfortunately, in making provision for the rights of third parties who claim interests in forfeited property, it purports to abrogate the right to a jury trial, a result questionable under the Seventh Amendment. *Cf. United States v. One 1976 Mercedes Benz*, 618 F.2d 453 (7th Cir. 1980) *(in rem* forfeiture of personality seized on land requires a jury trial). The bill passed the Senate on February 2, 1984, by a vote of 91 to 1. 139 Cong. Rec. § 759 (daily ed. Feb. 2, 1984). Its prospects in the House are uncertain.

70. For two views of forfeiture, *compare* Weiner, "Crime Must Not Pay: RICO Criminal Forfeiture in Perspective," 1981 *N. Ill. U. L. Rev.* 225 *with* Taylor, "Forfeiture under 18 U.S.C. § 1963–RICO's Most Powerful Weapon," 17 *Am. Crim. L. Rev.* 379 (1980). *See also* Webb and Turow, "RICO Forfeitures in Practice: A Prosecutorial Perspective," 52 *U. of Cinn. L. Rev.* 404 (1983).

9
What Should Be Done about Organized Crime?

Gerald E. Caiden

> Organized crime . . . is a quasi-public utility.
> Saul Alinsky

> The high level of lawlessness in American society is maintained by the fact that Americans desire to do so many things which they also desire to prohibit.
> Walter Lippmann

> Presumably this is an activity, i.e., prostitution, that is "bad" in some social sense, as witnessed by most universal legal prohibitions. . . . Yet for many potential buyers, the services of prostitutes are "goods" in the strict economic sense of this term; these buyers are willing to pay for these services in ordinary market transactions. From this it follows that monopoly organization is socially preferable to competitive organization precisely because of the restriction on total output that it fosters.
> James Buchanan

> Organized crime . . . is made up of career criminals of varied backgrounds and criminal specializations whose only common bond is the attainment of wealth, power, and influence by illegal means.
> Philip Manuel

> Organized crime seems to be such an integral part of the politics of American living that most Americans do not see it as a personal problem.
> Francis A.J. Ianni

> Organized crime is free enterprise at its freest.
> Hank Messick

> Organized crime is one of our queer ladders of social mobility.
> Daniel Bell

The first National Conference on Organized Crime held on November 8–9, 1979, at the University of Southern California, brought together various experts on organized crime from government, law enforcement, the mass media, and academia to review the current state of the art in combating organized crime and to suggest possible new directions that a nationwide strategy might take. It was predicated on the assumption that national efforts had been flagging just when organized crime seemed to have taken on extra dimensions. The situation was actually deteriorating, despite improved efforts after the President's Crime Commission to prosecute leading organized crime figures and to make the American public more aware of the costs of doing business with criminal organizations.

Virtually every speaker at the conference agreed that organized crime was a growing menace to American society and that national programs, where they existed, were inadequate, misdirected, and outmoded. Too many efforts were directed at pursuing the Mafia, that is, at prosecuting an alien conspiracy of organized predatory criminals in the belief that by lopping off the leadership, criminal organizations would fall apart and the foreign cancer within American society would be flushed out of the system. This was a highly fanciful idea of the nature of organized crime. Walter Lippmann had indicated in *Forum* as far back as 1931 that organized crime was a growth industry providing services that people desired but were inhibited by moral convention from acknowledging and legalizing. The underworld performed many services that respectable members of society wanted. Americans desired to do many things that they also desired to prohibit. Demand encouraged supply, and high risks were compensated by high returns. Huge profits could buy protection, finance entry into legitimate business, and eventually acquire respectability. Lopping off heads would not curtail demand, eliminate illegal enterprise (merely impose a reshuffling in personnel), or even disgrace the participants. Indeed, by some perverse logic, it would merely make folk heroes out of the criminal elite and induce aspiring members of the underprivileged to emulate them while taking greater precautions against being prosecuted and put out of business. A half-century after Lippmann's analysis, we still had not yet realized or understood its full significance.

Most conference participants were inclined to accept Lippmann's analysis and to take a quite different view of organized crime than commonly portrayed. They saw organized crime (or organized criminal activities or illegal enterprise or the underworld) as a permanent institution within American society with roots going back centuries. It was a social phenomenon in its own right that polite society had tended to ignore. As such, it was worthy of study like any other social phenomenon and could be studied scientifically, despite methodological problems caused by its conspiratorial, hidden, and unsavory nature. Such reliable studies that had been conducted indicated that its nature was not constant. As circumstances changed, it also changed, being capable of adaptation and transformation. Its activities, forms, and impacts had varied greatly even within recent history, and as a result of changes within contemporary society and perhaps because of the very studies referred to, it was currently being transformed in ways and shapes that even those who could be identified as its major movers could not properly identify or anticipate.

One thing above all else was certain. Organized crime, however defined, was different than it was a decade ago, and it was much more complex than we had been led to believe. Money and power were still the major attractions. Gangland, the mob, syndicates, coercive monopolies, bureaucratic conspiracies supplying illicit goods and services, employing subversive terrorist methods, engaging in a host of rackets, and using their ill-gotten untaxed profits to buy off prosecution and infiltrate legitimate institutions were still a substantial portion of organized crime. The participants still constituted a peculiar social system composed of various kinds of professional criminals. But prosecutions under Title IX of the Organized Crime Control Act of 1970 or RICO (Racketeer Influenced and Corrupt Organizations) alone had uncovered a slew of organized criminal activities that did not fall within traditional conceptions. Organized crime had moved on, become extremely sophisticated, entered new areas, taken on new forms, and had so infiltrated legitimate institutions that it was difficult to distinguish between legitimate and illegitimate business and to prosecute organized crime leaders under existing legal provisions. In short, organized crime had already outdistanced the current state of the art and was rapidly seizing new opportunities to enhance its profits and power.

Even if a nationwide strategy as proposed by the 1967 President's Crime Commission had not fallen victim to misdirection, indifference, and inaction, it would have had to be recast, altered, and thought out anew to cope with the changing nature of organized crime, the changing context in which organized crime operated, and the changing opportunities that new developments in technology, social values, and wealth were presenting to organized crime. The need for an effective national strategy was probably more pressing today than it had been fifteen years ago, and the more time it took to formulate and implement a nationwide strategy, the more difficult it would be to keep up with the changing nature of organized crime, the harder it would be to get a better grip on the problem, and the higher would be the costs to society in terms of maldistributed resources, intimidation, corruption, inflation, and the credibility of public institutions. The conference participants concluded that high priority should be given to devising a nationwide strategy to cope with organized crime as it was now and likely to be in the immediate future.

Among the principal thrusts that participants felt needed priority treatment were the following:

1. Investigate the causes and reasons why past nationwide strategies have failed and what needs to be done to reestablish an effective strategy.
2. Review the changing nature of organized crime to redefine the term and enable public authorities to reach a better understanding of the problem they confront.
3. Codify existing scientific research into organized crime and related areas completed in the United States and abroad so that a reliable research guide can be made available, indicating not only what has been done but what needs to be done.
4. Engage in exploratory studies of the world of organized crime (causes, nature, effects), measuring organized crime in the United States, connections between organized crime and public office, evaluating community prevention programs, and training law enforcement personnel to combat organized crime.

In short, what was needed was an ongoing research capability to assist in the formulation of a nationwide containment strategy. It will be no surprise if the 1983 President's Organized Crime Commission comes to the same conclusion. Its work will be sorely handicapped by the lack of appropriate ongoing research capability.

Organized Crime as a Taboo Subject

At the 1979 conference, I argued in "Confronting Taboos: Taking Organized Crime Out of the Closet" that all societies had taboo topics and that organized crime invariably was one of them. Nobody liked to admit that organized crime existed or could exist; people were discouraged from talking about it. Only a few open societies were honest and mature enough to admit that it existed, and, of these, the United States stood out. Yet even in this country, despite all the exposés, a veil of silence still persisted. Insufficient knowledge about organized crime existed to launch an effective national campaign against it.

To open up a thorough investigation into organized crime, several issues concerning the protection of sources, false pretenses, incompleteness, inaction, collusion, and intimidation needed to be squarely faced. These in turn raised compelling questions about the nature of U.S. society and whether organized crime was so pervasive that it could not be suppressed even if we knew how. Organized crime was sustained by collusion, corruption, and complacency. Too many of us wanted what organized crime was prepared to supply at a price we, as individuals, were willing to pay. It was already so big that established institutions had come to terms with it and were prepared to accommodate it as long as the public was kept in ignorance about its extent. We would rather not talk about such things because we knew we did wrong but were too weak to do anything about them. The taboo on organized crime covered our shame and weakness and hid the harm we did to the ethical basis of civilized society.

I accused academia of going along with the taboo and in so doing damaging its credibility and ignoring its moral obligation to remind society of things it would prefer not to know about. I referred to the current crop of textbooks on U.S. public policy and administration where one looked in vain for any account of public immorality, official lawlessness, bureaucratic deceit, administrative corruption, and the subversion of government by special interests. None of these topics was listed in any index. Not even Watergate and similar scandals had appreciably dented the impression that a benevolent government led by virtuous, selfless public leaders working in harmony with like-minded individuals from all walks of life was not doing everything humanly possible to bring about the good society in these United States. It seemed that the authors were reluctant to admit that anything but honesty and goodness prevailed in the conduct of public affairs. Maybe they believed that if they did not mention the seamy side, people would not know it existed and would not be tempted to tread wrong paths. Perhaps they wanted to do nothing that besmirched the international image of the United States or undermined public confidence in American bureaucracy. Yet their silence compounded the very conditions they wished to avoid because the truth could not be hidden so easily and problems of that kind were not in the habit of solving themselves.

Even without social and academic taboos, finding out about organized crime was difficult:

First, foreign information was meager and scattered. Only the richest international and national research institutions could collect it at all, and they had restrictive access policies for purely economic reasons or because they feared losing materials so difficult to acquire.

Second, domestic sources were usually confidential, if only to protect informants or prevent leakages during investigations or safeguard authorities from civil suits of maligned individuals. Access to information was further impeded by rivalry among public agencies that wanted sole credit and would not share what they knew. Access might also be legally restricted.

Third, public authorities responsible for public security and safety were notoriously secretive and tight-lipped. They did not necessarily believe in the public's right to know in this area. They were unsympathetic to academic research, investigating reporters, and their ilk, whom they distrusted, if not actively disliked. Once the information was out of their hands, they did not know how it would be used and would not take the risk of leakage.

Fourth, the way in which much information was collected and stored often meant that it could not be used. It was fragmentary, unsubstantiated, unproved, and otherwise inadequate. There were not many reliable sources, and students of organized crime were very much at the mercy of the same published evidence.

Fifth, little encouragement was given to expanding research frontiers. Crime was low on the totem pole of research and development. It had none of the glamour of medicine, physics, or biochemistry or the academic status of mathematics, law, or philosophy. Even in the social sciences, it ranked low. Within that low ranking, organized crime was not favored. Students were persuaded to look at some other area where research funds and support were available and where the methodological problems were less daunting.

Sixth, the methodological problems were crippling. No two experts could agree on how to define organized crime, let alone what it encompassed or how to discover meaningful data. It was a conspiratorial activity, and there were personal risks in penetrating and revealing conspiracies.

All of these inhibiting factors reinforced whatever taboos existed and combined in effect to present overwhelming odds against successful exploration and as such to constitute a prohibition.

To summarize, good reasons existed why organized crime stayed in the closet. There were a great many other topics that occupied people's attention, that were more central to their concerns, and that commanded official support for investigation. Relatively few persons were willing or able to bring organized crime out of the closet, at least not for the personal risks involved, the official discouragements encountered, and the practical obstacles that had to be overcome. As it was illegal and conspiratorial, investigation ought to be left to public authorities, which could better protect themselves and were in a better position to uncover the facts by matching organized crime in sophistication without being compromised. Simplest of all was not to get involved, ignoring the phenomenon and pretending it did not exist.

Exposing Organized Crime

In this, I was wrong. From that time, I began to collect newspaper clippings on organized crime and from that source alone soon had amassed a sizable data bank on most aspects of the subject. I taught some courses in the area and sent out inexperienced and untrained undergraduates to investigate organized crime in the local community. Almost without exception they came up with new evidence and opened paths that led into areas that I had never expected.

People had few reservations talking about their experiences, and although we kept our sources confidential, we were able to induce more extensive follow-up investigations by local mass media and law enforcement leading to extensive exposés of organized crime operations and practices and to some prosecutions. Organized crime, we concluded, was not a taboo subject at all or to a much less extent than I had supposed in the late 1970s. Anyone who really wanted to know about it in the United States could, if persistent enough, find out a great deal by reading official investigations and pop crime authors, consulting the handful of textbooks on the subject, clipping relevant articles out of major newspapers and periodicals, attending a few trials of organized crime figures, and talking with local law enforcement investigators.

In this way, we had exposed for ourselves such topics as the following:

Transactions in the underground economy.

The maintenance of the underclass beyond welfare support.

Foreign routes of narcotics traffic into the United States.

Open borders, airports, and harbors.

Professional sports.

Supply of narcotics to local schools and law firms.

Male prostitution and pornography.

Campaigns for legalized gambling.

Computer fraud in banking, insurance, and real estate.

Labor racketeering, corrupt unions, and rip-off fringe benefits schemes.

Contracting in hazardous waste disposal, garbage collection, and defense industries.

Pimping.

Corruption.

Kickbacks.

We expanded our notions of organized crime from the traditional concerns such as narcotics and prostitution to corporate crime and public maladministration, for we became increasingly convinced that legitimate business was more involved than we had imagined, that public maladministration and incompetence was much to blame, and that political, legal, and judicial corruption was responsible for inaction. We could name names, places, dates, action, and transactions, few of which had been subject to criminal prosecution, and we came to know of certain public officials who had been on the take for a long time, who regularly consorted with known organized crime figures, and who had used their organized crime connections to gain advancement in their public careers.

In the process, we raised several issues and questions that still lack ready convincing or definitive answers.

1. Protection of sources. To uncover organized crime, investigators have to associate with underworld figures or participate themselves in conspiratorial activities. When can they legitimately refuse to reveal their sources? To what extent can they promise or be promised immunity in exchange for their information? Presumably if they are compelled in the public interest to reveal all, they can never be used in that capacity again, they place both their informants and themselves in jeopardy, and they may have to be protected for life by changing identities.

2. False pretenses. To obtain evidence of illegality, investigators have to disguise their intentions and deceive informants as to their purpose. They cannot reveal who they are or what they are up to. To what extent should such unethical practices be tolerated? What credibility should be placed on information obtained by deceit? If they were to reveal themselves and their intentions, they would not obtain any information at all.

3. Incompleteness. Suspicions cannot be substantiated when

much of the incriminating evidence is deliberately destroyed or otherwise unobtainable. Even with the best will, investigators are unlikely to obtain a complete picture. Some distortion is unavoidable. The minimizers say that what they found was all there was to find; they are proud of the job they did. The maximizers say that what they found was merely the tip of the iceberg; they want more resources to reveal yet more. How are false impressions to be curtailed? How are the different interpretations to be reconciled?

4. Inaction. Investigators expect that some notice will be taken of their findings and that some action will be taken. But because of the need to protect sources, reluctance to act on evidence falsely obtained, and incompleteness of the information, action is inadvisable. How is the morale of committed investigators maintained? What is to prevent leakages that forewarn organized crime or condemn inactivity? Failure to act makes investigators cynical and adds evidence to the belief that someone is being sheltered.

5. Collusion. Investigators cannot be expected to show objective detachment at all times. They have their own private reasons for pursuing organized crime. No doubt some see their work as a moral crusade against the forces of darkness just as others seize new opportunities for self-aggrandizement. If the rewards of organized crime are exorbitant, the risks of detection low, and the penalties on conviction lenient, how are the temptations to collude to be resisted? Collusion is profitable, and organized crime can afford to pay steep prices for cooperation.

6. Intimidation. Organized crime is well supported, or it would barely survive. Many people benefit from it. Many others are intimidated by it. Already beyond the law, it has few moral scruples in dealing with those who give it offense. In addition, organized crime can draw on its allies in legitimate institutions to block action when direct intimidation fails. Just how conscious are legitimate institutions of working on behalf of organized crime? How can investigators be protected from intimidation and suppression? To whom do potential whistle-blowers appeal when all around them are compromised by organized crime?

Clearly the exposure of organized crime raises deeper societal issues. It bares the very soul of society. Take, for instance, two other dimensions, one economic and the other moral, one concerning the development of a black economy or a countereconomy, the other concerning the destruction of traditional ethical standards. The existence of illegal enterprise and the fusion of illegitimate and legitimate business create an extralegal or black economy distinct from the regular economy, beyond governmental regulation and possibly working at cross-purposes to official economic policy. In the United States, for example, an income from all sources amounting to $220 billion would give organized crime a budget roughly equal to the U.S. Department of Defense and well over double that of the largest multinational business corporations. How does the black economy differ from the regular economy, and how does it interact? Who really pays for illegal goods and services, and how are costs passed on? To what extent does organized crime redistribute income and capital, influence investment patterns and savings, alter trade flows, and disturb foreign exchange markets?

While organized crime may be pure entrepreneurship unfettered by noneconomic considerations, its ethic of "making it," its rip-off mentality, its disregard of social costs, its crass materialism, its reliance on intimidation and violence, all run counter to the basic moral tenets of Western society. The contrasting ethical system creates conflict and confusion, corrupts the socialization process, and turns traditional Judeo-Christian morality upside down. It mocks social responsibility. It deliberately caters to the baser instincts and gratifies aberrations. It cheapens life. It worships power. Where does organized crime take society? What is its image of the good society? What future does it envisage for humanity?

The exposure of organized crime makes society look closely at itself. What is portrayed may not be at all flattering to social self-images. It will show many blemishes in the nature of prevailing ethical standards and morals, in the state of the laws, lawlessness, and law enforcement, in the conduct of public business and official behavior, in the effectiveness of social controls, government regulation, and communal policing, and in the willingness of public authorities, established institutions, and professional crime fighters to tackle organized crime. It paints a dismal, frightening, and disillusioning picture. Either we leave it as it is and permit organized crime to continue to gnaw at society, or we do something about it, reminding people that the good society is unattainable until organized crime is eradicated. They cannot afford to go on being victimized. If history tells us anything, it is that organized crime contaminates and destroys all that it touches and eventually rots even the greatest empires.

Hollywood showed the world the ugly side of organized crime in this country during prohibition. That it still persists comes as surprise to those who believe that it belonged in the past. What surprises them more is the complacency toward it that generally prevails, which is attributed to traditional American tolerance, free expression, and enterprise, a permissiveness rarely found elsewhere. They are amazed by the easy access to illegal goods and services supplied by organized crime, but most choose not to indulge, not to get involved, out of moral disgust or fear of the consequences should they get caught or drawn into something they do not really understand.

Most Americans also avoid dealing with organized crime when they can. Unfortunately they cannot always recognize it for what it is, or they succumb to spasmodic lapses. Because of its various guises and the increasingly sophisticated manner in which organized crime operates, they do not know with whom they deal. If they do realize, they prefer to act as if they did not. While they prefer to ignore organized crime, organized crime does not ignore them. It is always trying to expand its operations and to explore new markets wherever high returns can be made. Since prohibition, which ended in the legitimization of many illegal entrepreneurs linked to underground mafias supplying other illegal markets, narcotics seem to have become the most profitable and widespread illegal business, with single shipments valued in the hundreds of millions of dollars and a distribution network covering virtually every community across the country. Other illegal markets, such as gambling, prostitution, and fencing, seem to have experienced in real dollar terms similar if not such spectacular growth. The profits and connections made in these traditional organized crime markets have enabled organized crime to exploit new markets, such as pornography, arson, and waste disposal, and to trade in legal markets without distinction, through complex mixed organizations.

If street gangs, corporate crime, and computer crime are included within the definition of organized crime, then the presence of organized crime affects Americans in more ways than they care to know. It adds to the costs of doing business, costs that are passed on to consumers in higher prices. It results in grievous harm to millions who get ensnared. It promotes violence and theft. It corrupts the political system. It perverts the legal system. It subverts public policy. It supports sick life-styles. It diverts a substantial part of national income, perhaps as high as 15 percent, into the wrong hands. It diminishes the quality of life by casting such fear that scared people feel they have to hire private police, reduce their outside activities, and lock themselves in their homes. In short, organized crime shapes American society in ways that most Americans do not want it shaped.

Worse still, because of its strength, it prevails against their will. They feel powerless to contain it.

Current State of Ignorance

The conspiratorial nature of organized criminal activities will always hinder our abilities to measure with accuracy their scope, extent, and impact. They are part of an underground in our society that is difficult to explore in depth without self-incrimination. Probably no one can fathom the whole of it. The best we can do is to find out what we can from various bits and pieces and extrapolate from them what the rest may look like. In this way we get to know something about criminal organizations—how they operate, who is supposed to mastermind their activities, what they do to avoid or evade prosecution, and how much power they exercise. In this way, too, we cannot avoid wild generalizations drawn from scanty evidence or myths based on unrepresentative samples or false leads (provided by clever criminals to disguise their real practices) masquerading as truth.

We are waging a losing battle. Whatever we do, organized crime is always one step ahead. Criminal organizations know before time what we intend to do. They can reorganize and readjust to meet new threats. In time they expand their activities, seizing every new opportunity that occurs to develop new markets for illegal goods and services. They penetrate further into legitimate business and established institutions so that it becomes increasingly difficult to single them out. They grow more sophisticated, employing high-quality professional talent and the most advanced technology. They combine to amass wealth and power. They will go on doing so as long as we know so little about them and our containment efforts remain so piecemeal, haphazard, fragmentary, uncoordinated, imprecise, ill defined, and compromised.

Clearly a new approach is called for if we are to get a firm handle on organized crime. We need to encourage solid, scientific research into the underworld. We need to know how it developed, why it persists, and what directions it is likely to take. We need to identify its forms, boundaries, and where it dovetails into the familiar. We need to know what goes on within it and to find out whether it matches our preconceptions, hunches, and assessments. We need a better understanding of illegal, unethical, and immoral activities. In particular, we need to study extralegal market systems and what is involved in the supply of illegal goods and services. We need to know what constitutes illegal enterprise and how it differs from legitimate business. We need to know more about institutionalized racketeering, the structure of rackets, and the composition of racketeers and their victims. Currently we are groping in the dark and grateful for any illlumination. We do not know enough to tell whether we are going after the right targets, whether we are putting our efforts into the right places, whether we are doing the right things, whether we could attain better results using different approaches, and whether, paradoxically, our containment efforts may be contributing to the problem of organized crime in society.

These points are hardly new. They predate the Wickersham Commission. They have been repeated often enough. In recent years, they have been emphasized by the President's Crime Commission and subsequent bodies commissioned to formulate a national containment strategy. A report on federal efforts issued by the U.S. General Accounting Office (GGD-77-17) was particularly critical of current failures to get to grips with the central issues. But this attention has been beneficial in several respects. The taboo on organized crime has been dispelled. Congress has been stirred to pass legislation and provide funds strengthening national efforts to deal with organized crime. More funds have been allocated for research into substantive areas of organized crime, such as loan-sharking and gambling. Effort has been spent on defining operational standards and guidelines to contain organized crime. The number of successful prosecutions has increased. The public has been warned of methods used by organized crime to attract new victims. Nevertheless, these creditable advances have barely made a dent.

Given that virtually every aspect of organized crime needs researching, the question becomes one of priorities. Should we focus on criminal activities that are organized or on criminal organizations that provide illegal goods and services? Research into the different extralegal markets—narcotics, loan-sharking, prostitution, gambling, labor racketeering—would reveal much about the demand side—the clients, the customers, the victims—as well as the supply side—the illegitimate entrepreneurs, the unsuspecting legitimate businesses, and the compromised intermediaries. It would probably reveal different rates of profitability and risk, indicating where ill-gotten gains were the highest and how they compared with the social costs of illegtimate enterprise. Research into the different kinds of criminal organization behind illegal transactions (multinationals, domesticate syndicates, and specialized local rings) would uncover their trade secrets such as supply sources, distribution channels, management practices, and means of protection. It would aid prosecution and might indicate how they could be made unprofitable, stripped of power, and pushed out of business. Together they might reveal why criminal organizations are soon replaced, why they are so often protected by established institutions, and where distinctions between proper and improper business practices can be drawn.

Undoubtedly substantive research on these lines is badly needed and should be encouraged. But it is costly, controversial, time-consuming, and demanding. It cannot be hurried along. It has to be properly thought out and carefully executed. Complex methodological and operational problems cannot be short cut. A pool of qualified researchers and adequate research designs cannot be miraculously conjured up. To succeed, it needs a substantial national commitment, solid backing from all levels of government and from business, and guaranteed long-term funding shielded from political haggling. Otherwise much of it will suffer a similar fate to that of past research when many starts were made but few were completed because of poor research designs and inadequate research support. Those that were completed had little impact on public policy. Either the projects had deteriorated into research for research's sake rather than meeting the needs of the law enforcement community or by the time they had been completed, they were already out of date, and interest had been shifted to something else. In brief, even if such research were done properly, there is no guarantee that the findings will be heeded or incorporated into containment strategies. Why is this so?

Common Sense and Organized Crime

Common sense suggests that the higher the level of demand for illegal goods and services, whatever their form and however defined, the greater the temptation (and potential rewards) to supply them. Demand can be cut off only by redesigning human beings or by so intimidating them that they are too frightened to participate in illegal markets. Supply can be cut off only by employing draconian measures and institutionalizing a police state. For a liberal society, the price of elimination is too high. Some organized crime has to be expected and tolerated. The question is how much, in what form, and where. Because people indulge spasmodically, organized crime will be available somewhere, near somebody's home (or somebody else's home), or in specially designated areas (red light districts, resort casinos), discreetly, where it does not give offense. In this way, it can be ignored as long as nobody important gets offended enough to complain, things do not get out of hand, nobody gets seriously hurt, and the illegal entrepreneurs are reminded from time to time that they must pay something back for continuing in illegal business. A little genteel hypocrisy is the price of freedom.

This common-sense approach to organized crime would be more acceptable if it did not contain serious flaws in three major assumptions: that public complaints against organized crime excesses are acted on, that law enforcement remains vigilant and intervenes when the unofficial rules of the game are broken, and that organized crime keeps within the unofficial rules. In contemporary American society, none of these assumptions is valid.

The political system is dulled to public complaints. Because much organized crime is disguised and secret, the public is unaware of its extent, particularly corporate crime and racketeering. The employment of front organizations and the integration of illegal and legal business blurs the boundary of organized crime. Unless skilled in organized crime detection, many people are oblivious of the organized crime around them, and even if suspicious, they cannot produce any evidence. To substantiate their charges, they need to be inside. When on the inside, they have to overcome real fears of self-incrimination, retaliation, and social disapproval of ratting. People who should complain do not complain or withdraw their complaints when they do. The public's voice is muted. Anyway, what does one complain about, to whom does one complain, and how representative are the complaint and the complainant?

For organized crime, there are many different publics. Each form of organized crime has different audiences and is tolerated differently. Narcotics are viewed differently from loan-sharking or arson or protection rackets. Some groups intolerant of some forms of organized crime are tolerant of other forms, and their vehemence varies. Parents may view pornography and narcotics differently for their children and for themselves. Respectable businessmen may not tolerate prostitution in their residences but may expect it in hotels. Public complaints are difficult to interpret; volume is not necessarily commensurate with intensity of feeling. To complicate matters, there are counterclaims to every complaint, some more vociferous than others. Which lobby should prevail? The public's voice is confused.

The publics complain as best they know how. Many do not know how or to whom to complain, or because they believe nobody will listen to them, they do not bother to complain. Thus the inarticulate, dispossessed, and underprivileged are disadvantaged compared with the influential who are in touch with the powerful, make their views known, and expect prompt action. Notwithstanding, complaints are newsworthy and mass media publicize what they pick up, within the limits of self-censorship. What one newspaper will publish, another will not. What one editor will sensationalize, another will play down. Photographic evidence is best, whether real or faked. There is nothing like a film of a crime in progress or a confession from a self-incriminating criminal. All this distorts the public's voice.

For the political system, the public's voice is muted, confused, and distorted. It is difficult to pick out what should be taken seriously. To overreact and treat all complaints equally will provoke public opinion the other way and drive organized crime further underground where it is harder to get at. As it is better to have to increase pressure rather than relax it, so it pays to act cautiously and even to act deaf on occasions when repression is likely to aggravate significant publics. Consequently the level of organized crime in any society is likely to be higher than people want simply because they do not know all the facts and the political system is reluctant to misinterpret public complaints, and certain forms of organized crime are more likely to be sheltered (or conversely prosecuted) than others, according to the different strengths of the publics involved and the ebb and flow of public opinion.

Law enforcement is compromised. The political system knows about organized crime, yet it is not supposed to know enough to repress. It permits what organized crime the public (or publics) wants insofar as there are no compelling complaints to force intervention. The law is still the law and is employed as and when necessary, but enforcement is discretionary, which means in practice arbitrary and discriminatory. This is both legally and morally confusing. It causes hysteria in law enforcement circles. When nobody complains, is there a crime? When is a victim a victim? Is there such a thing as a victimless crime? When nobody complains, who protects the public interest? Just what kind of modus vivendi can exist between law enforcement and organized crime without compromising law enforcement? Yet law enforcement is supposed to turn a blind eye at least to certain kinds of organized crime if the public or specific publics do not mind and violence, destruction, pain, and theft are minimal.

Once organized crime and law enforcement coexist, they must consort. Law enforcement is supposed to know all about organized crime just in case community pressures build, and it is enjoined to act. This entails the penetration of organized crime, the use of informers, and surveillance of organized crime figures (or illegal business) and their clients. Contrary to its ethics and professional values, law enforcement to some extent has to engage in dirty tricks, plant undercover agents, contract with finks, and generally liaise with presumed targets. The legal and illegal converge. All too easily, the unidentifiable line can be crossed. The hunters come to sympathize with the hunted and then join in the conduct of illegal business as a partner. Vice and narcotics squads are notoriously prone to compromise and subversion, but insurance assessors and business regulators are just as susceptible. Supposed antagonists come to share too much.

On the other hand, where law enforcement tries to distance itself from organized crime, it may deliberately foster for public consumption a myth of organized crime. It may invent mafias where none exist. It may exaggerate the penetration of organized crime in legitimate business. In this way, law enforcement can justify its existence and demand more resources to keep up its fight against the underworld. Many things that cannot otherwise be explained can conveniently be attributed to secret mafias in high places. It is probably no coincidence that many organized crime buffs are found in law enforcement. If organized crime did not exist, it would have to be invented. Thus, although organized crime is more pervasive than the public knows, it may well be below what law enforcement estimates.

The coexistence of law enforcement and organized crime has a civilizing effect. A mutual respect exists between them. The one never knows when it might need the other. They work in close proximity. They are not strangers. Open warfare serves nobody's interest; it can work only to the detriment of all. Exceptions can be found on both sides, but such zealots are embarrassing, and they are soon dropped. To succeed on either side, one must accept the rules built around coexistence and just be smart (or smarter) at playing them. But whereas law enforcement must keep to the law, organized crime does not.

Organized crime exceeds the unofficial rules. To expect criminals to stick to any rules, official or not, is folly. They already operate on the other side of law. It may be in their self-interest to acknowledge certain limitations expected by law enforcement, but to conduct illegal business, intimidation is their weapon because they cannot call on the legal system to enforce contracts and remedy misplaced trust. Superficially courteous, compassion is reserved for intimates, not business associates. How far organized crime is willing to go is an individual affair. The unscrupulous stop at nothing. To their victims, it makes little difference what criminals do personally and what they order others to do. Nobody can accurately estimate how many people are killed or maimed by organized crime in a year or how much property is destroyed and stolen. Even conservative estimates are alarming. Organized crime is so smart, it gets away most of the time. In short, it does well by playing by the rules it wants and breaking them when it can.

Besides exploiting every possible loophole, organized crime possesses a trump card: it can go over the head of law enforcement and buy off prosecution. Organized crime penetrates wherever it can—into corporate headquarters, top legal firms, legislatures, governors' offices, mayors' offices, prisons, courts, police—and in such key industries as communications, airlines, computers, trucking, hotels and restaurants, and construction, wherever decisions crucial to its operations are made. Corruption tips the scales in its favor against public opinion. It is no secret that organized crime has ruled some important major cities, perhaps some major states as well, and it has ruled some important government and corporate offices too, including law enforcement. Even without the help of local political machines, organized crime appears to be moving rapidly into new territory in the public sector and aiming for local control of waste disposal, garbage collection, prepaid health plans, and public works maintenance.

If all this was not enough, organized crime purchases respectability. Money is money; that which is illegally gained can be legally spent on financing legitimate businesses, investments, education, election campaigns, and club memberships. Corporate criminals deck business halls of fame. Liquor merchants, gun runners, hoteliers, mine owners, and the like who have profited from illegal markets have little difficulty getting into *Who's Who* and *The Social Register*. Even indictments and imprisonment for organized crime do not blemish relatives and associates. Sociologists call it upward mobility, and historians of organized crime refer to Italian, Irish, Jewish, and black mafias as avenues of upward social mobility, not of private interest exploiting the public weal against the public interest. A truly open society welcomes everyone and admires those who make it in their chosen professions.

While common sense suggests that in the short run nothing much will be effective against communal tolerance of organized crime, it does indicate long-run strategies that could be effective in containing organized crime and possibly minimizing its social dysfunctions.

First, political corruption has to be reduced, and to do this, corruption in law enforcement has to be eliminated. Clean law enforcement can do much to cleanse the political system. Without political corruption, organized crime loses much of its protection.

Second, the strengthening of professionalism in law enforcement should limit any compromise with organized crime, offset inclinations to go along with public complacency, and demonstrate greater initiative and leadership in the battle against organized crime. When the public does not know the facts, professional law enforcement, which knows them better, should in the name of public safety lead, not follow, public opinion. Professional law enforcement should not rely on some other body's taking the initiative, for others may be much more compromised.

Third, the public has to be educated on the full extent of organized crime and won over to intensified efforts to reduce the more intolerable forms. The public has a naive and distorted view of organized crime and needs to be educated on the facts. In this, organized crime cannot be treated as being homogeneous. It is composed of many different illegal markets, each probably catering to a different clientele, each possibly operating separately, each requiring different containment strategies. Arson has a great deal to do with overvalued insurance. Cocaine is related to the ease of access into the United States.

Fourth, if any impact is to be made, fragmented, isolated, and piecemeal efforts have to be combined into a more effective strike force. Organized crime is a national problem that has to be tackled on a national basis. Local efforts are nullified by disjointed and uneven campaigns. A national campaign does not necessarily require federal leadership, but it does require considerable cooperation at all levels of government in all parts of the country, cooperation that seems difficult to achieve.

Fifth, illegal markets—if they do work on a market model—need to be made unprofitable. The profits have to be taken out of illegal business, or at least considerably reduced, so that demand does not breed supply so readily. Some illegal markets may have to be legalized, as in the case of prohibition. In others, the penalties for illegal trading may have to be increased, as in the case of racketeering. In a few, the crime may have to be carefully redefined, as in the case of pornography, or better monitored and regulated, as in the case of gambling.

Sixth, more scientific research into organized crime and its impact on society is needed. Mass media do their part in exposing organized crime. What is lacking to the public is sufficient hard analysis. How pervasive is the underground economy in the United States? How is it composed? What are the trends in each segment of illegal business? What are the growth markets? What strategies have worked best in containing organized crime? Where do containment efforts need to be concentrated? What are the major obstacles that have to be overcome, and what needs to be done to overcome them? Has organized crime become so entrenched in American society that it is indispensable and cannot now be reduced without causing serious economic dislocation? How big a problem is it? Is it a problem that needs to be tackled immediately?

Seventh, analysis is only as good as the sources of intelligence, which in this country involve many different agencies at every level of government jealously guarding their territories against encroachment and duplicating efforts. Yet they do not cover the whole scene and reveal little in what they do cover, handicapped by lack of adequate funds, the threat of libel suits, and the slow nature of investigation. Each form of organized crime resembles a giant jigsaw puzzle with many pieces missing and others so scattered that no pattern can be seen. The ability of the criminal intelligence community in keeping track of developments in organized crime needs to be improved within a code of rules that protects privacy and respects human rights. It should not be beyond legal capability to devise such a code.

Eighth, every effort should be made to build and retain law enforcement professionalism in organized crime. At present, much painstaking expertise is quickly dissipated. Worse still, such talent is recruited by organized crime and used against law enforcement; investigators join the very groups they have been investigating. What is needed is a long-term commitment to the investigation of organized crime and careful research in evaluating control techniques in specific industries susceptible to organized crime penetration.

If organized crime is a functioning institution within American society, condoned in many ways both by the public and the government, then it cannot be treated as something analogous to street crime or white-collar crime. "If it is to be attacked, it can only be done so effectively if it is regarded as a pervasive social and cultural phenomenon and not solely as a matter for police action," concluded Michael Aguirre and Brendan Nagle from the papers presented to USC's 1979 Organized Crime Conference. We may find that organized crime is a pragmatic response to moral ambivalence in a democratic society where consensus cannot be achieved in the political system. If this is so, the commnon-sense approach, with all its faults, has much to commend it.

Index

About the Contributors

David J. Bellis is a lecturer in political science and public administration at the University of Southern California. He has also taught at the University of California, Los Angeles; California State University, Long Beach; and Long Beach City College. He is a two-term elected city councilman in the city where he resides.

G. Robert Blakey is professor of law at Notre Dame Law School, a position he has held since 1980. In 1977–1978, Blakey served as chief counsel and staff director of the House Select Committee on Assassination and in 1969 1973 he was chief counsel of the Subcommittee on Criminal Law and Prosecution of the U.S. Senate.

Clifford L. Karchmer is a research scientist at Battelle Human Affairs Research Centers in Washington, D.C. Mr. Karchmer has been director of the Massachusetts Organized Crime Control Council and operations director of the National Center on White Collar Crime. His research interests lie in the fields of narcotics control, financial crime, and arson.

Mark Kleiman is senior analyst, Center for Criminal Justice, Harvard University Law School, and president, BOTEC Analysis Corporation, which provides management analysis services to law enforcement agencies. Mr. Kleiman was director of Policy and Management Analysis in the Criminal Division of the Department of Justice, 1979–1983.

Michael D. Maltz is professor of criminal justice and quantitative methods at the University of Illinois in Chicago. He is the author of *Recidivism* (1984) and numerous chapters and articles on methodological and statistical research in criminal justice.

Peter Reuter is a senior economist at the Rand Corporation in Washington, D.C. He is the author of *Disorganized Crime: The Economics of the Visible Hand*. His current research focuses on tax evasion and the economics of illicit drug markets.

About the Editors

Herbert E. Alexander is professor of political science at the University of Southern California and since 1958 has been director of the Citizens' Research Foundation. He received the B.S. from the University of North Carolina, the M.A. from the University of Connecticut, and the Ph.D. in political science from Yale University. Dr. Alexander has taught at Princeton University, the University of Pennsylvania, and Yale University. He also has held a number of government posts, including executive director of the president's Commission on Campaign Costs and consultant to the Office of Federal Elections at the General Accounting Office. In 1973–1974, Dr. Alexander undertook a consultancy with the U.S. Senate Select Committee on Presidential Campaign Activities.

Dr. Alexander has written extensively on matters relating to money in politics. In addition to his series of books on the financing of presidential election campaigns since 1960—including the latest, *Financing the 1980 Election*—he has authored *Financing Politics: Money, Elections, and Political Reform*, now in its third edition, and *Money in Politics*. He is the editor of *Campaign Money: Reform and Reality in the States* and coauthor of *The Federal Election Campaign Act: After a Decade of Political Reform*.

Gerald E. Caiden, a native of London, England, graduated from the London School of Economics and Political Science. He has served on the faculties of the University of London (1957–1959), Carleton University (1959–1960), the Australian National University (1961–1966), the Hebrew University (1966–1968), University of California, Berkeley (1968–1971), Haifa University (1971–1975), and the University of Southern California (1975 to the present). He has published more than twenty books and monographs and over one hundred journal articles, has acted as editorial consultant to several leading journals in the field of public administration, and has served as a reader for notable publishing houses. He has acted as consultant, researcher, and administrator to a wide variety of public organizations ranging from the World Bank and the United Nations Organization to local authorities and public utilities. He is known best for his research in administrative reform and organizational diagnosis.